'A very <u>IMPORTANT</u> book, encouraging us all to celebrate, as it does, the uniqueness and gift of our own and others' <u>DIFFERENCES</u>, while recognising all of that which we share in common.' – Michael D. Higgins, President of Ireland

First published in Great Britain in 2020 by Wren & Rook

ISBN: 978 1 5263 6333 6

10 9 8 7 6

MIX
Paper from
responsible sources
FSC
www.fsc.org   FSC® C104740

Wren & Rook
An imprint of
Hachette Children's Group
Part of Hodder & Stoughton
Carmelite House
50 Victoria Embankment
London EC4Y 0DZ

A Hachette UK Company
www.hachette.co.uk
www.hachettechildrens.co.uk

Publishing Director: Debbie Foy
Commissioning Editor: Laura Horsley
Editor: Phoebe Jascourt
Art Director: Laura Hambleton
Senior Designer: Sophie Gordon
Designed by Thy Bui

Printed in the United Kingdom

SINÉAD BURKE
ILLUSTRATED BY NATALIE BYRNE

BREAK the MOULD

wren
&rook

For my Mam, Dad, Natasha,
Niamh, Chris and Chloe.

Without you, none of this would
be possible. I love you.

CONTENTS

'BREAK THE MOULD'

I wonder whether you've ever thought to yourself: I would love to stand out. To do things differently. To make a difference. To change the world. To break the mould. But you figured – no, that's impossible.

In many ways, that was my story. Or, it could have been.

When I was younger, I wanted to be a teacher, I wanted to work in fashion and I wanted to change the world. But I'm a little person. I have dwarfism, which is a physical disability that means my arms and legs are a little bit shorter than most people. Growing up, there weren't very many teachers, or writers, or fashion designers, or activists who were disabled like me.

Not seeing someone who looked like me in the places I longed to be, meant that I used to think that my dreams were impossible. But from my earliest days, my parents encouraged me to believe that I could do anything that I dreamed of. They told me that I might have to find a different way to achieve my dream, but it wasn't impossible. Just because it hadn't been done before, it didn't mean that I couldn't be the first.

I went on to become the first little person to be on the cover of *Vogue*, a monthly fashion and lifestyle magazine. I was the first little person to attend the Met Gala – a very fancy fundraising ball where lots of celebrities get dressed up in amazing costumes. I created the first little person doll and the first little person mannequin, because when I was growing up, there were never any toys or shop mannequins that looked like me. I introduced the word for little person into the Irish dictionary and into Irish Sign Language and I am the first little person to ever advise the President of Ireland. I'm part of a group of people, called the Council of State, who he calls on whenever there is a big decision to be made.

I was able to fulfil my dreams. Now I want to help you fulfil yours.

D R E A M S

PERMISSION TO DREAM

The act of making a dream a reality does not happen overnight. It takes time, effort and perseverance, but YOU can make it happen. You can discover and create your own dreams and I want to show you how. Let's rewind and step back in time to my very first day of school ...

I was SO nervous. I wanted to make friends and I wanted to fit in. I looked different from the other girls in my class. I was concerned that they might not know how to talk to me, or what to say. I was worried that their nervousness might have meant that they wouldn't talk to me at all. I decided to introduce myself, to put everyone at ease. So I told them a story about me.

It was just a few lines. I practised it at home in front of the mirror and felt a mix of fear and excitement. I walked into the classroom and everyone looked at me. They all wore the same clothes: a bright blue jumper, shirt, bowtie and pinafore. I wore them too and in our uniform, I looked like the other girls, just smaller.

The teacher told the class that I was their new classmate and asked me to say hello. It was my moment. Standing in front of them, I waved and smiled. I took a deep breath and said,

'Hi, my name is SINÉAD. I am four years old. I have ACHONDROPLASIA. That's spelled a-c-h-o-n-d-r-o-p-l-a-s-i-a. It means that I'm a LITTLE PERSON and I can do most things just like you.'

It was not only my first day of school, it was also my fourth birthday.

The teacher had a look on her face that said she wasn't expecting a speech. It was the kind of look where an adult is trying their best not to smile, but they can't control it and a grin stretches across their face.

The class shouted,

'WELCOME SINÉAD'

and over-emphasised every syllable in my name. With so many voices, it sounded like Shin-aye-yed. It didn't matter, I was part of the class, I would spend eight years in a classroom with these girls and, already, I felt accepted. I was one of them.

They had made small changes to help me feel comfortable. At the back of the classroom, we hung up our coats, hats and scarves on bright, colourful hooks. Mine was at the end of the row and much lower than the rest. The ability to hang my coat up, on my own, might seem trivial or unimportant, but it allowed me to be a student in the same way as everyone else.

In my classroom, there were thirty spaces for children to sit and every table and chair looked the same - wooden with red metal bars for the legs. My seat was at the front of the room, my table and chair were identical to everyone else's, but smaller. The legs had been shortened, and they were just the right height for me to be able to sit down, without using a footstool and without having to ask anyone for help.

I loved school. In the classroom it seemed anything was possible. There was a playhouse nestled in the corner and inside, there were costumes and lots of accessories. I remember spending hours dressing up, sometimes as a doctor wearing a white coat over my uniform, with a stethoscope around my neck. Other times wearing a chef's hat and jacket, and every now and then, wearing a hard hat and a high-vis jacket like a construction worker. I loved to play, dream and imagine all the possibilities of who I could be and what I could do when I left school.

Then I would zig-zag from the playhouse to the classroom library where I would run my fingers along the spines of the books. I loved turning the pages and escaping to a different world. Learning about princes and princesses, countries and cultures that I could only dream of experiencing. It was bliss.

That first day, I didn't want school to end. When the bell rang for us to go home, I left the classroom dragging my feet and my schoolbag, desperate to spend a few more minutes there.

I had made up my mind. Bursting out the school doors, I told my parents that I wanted to go to school for ever. When I was old enough, I wanted to be a teacher. They didn't hesitate, not for a moment. Smiling brightly, they both looked at me and said, 'Great!'.

I often wonder how my mam and dad felt at that moment. They had worked with the school to create the coat hook and my table and chair at a smaller height. Already it was obvious that the classroom wasn't designed for a little person as a student, so could a little person be a teacher? It would be difficult to reach things, to see all of the children, and as none of my teachers looked like me, maybe that meant it was impossible. Maybe I couldn't be a teacher. My mam and dad were calm, but I wonder if they were thinking about this and asking themselves these questions?

You see, we live in a world where there are often ASSUMPTIONS about what a person CAN or CANNOT do or be, because they are DIFFERENT.

When there are no role models, or people who look like you, already achieving your dreams, it's easy to think that your dreams are impossible. But that's rarely true.

When I told my parents that I wanted to be a teacher, they didn't accept those biases, which are assumptions about what or how something should be. My mam and dad gave me permission to dream.

My life might be very different without that moment because sometimes, all you need is someone to believe in you. That someone could be a parent, a grandparent, a brother, a sister, a cousin, a friend or it could be you, believing in yourself. We all need someone to tell us that

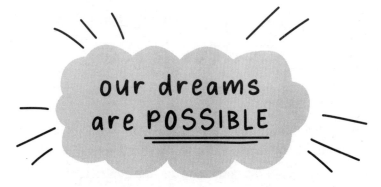

our dreams
are POSSIBLE

and to remind us how brilliant and unique we each are.

THIS BOOK

Now I'm passing on that message.

I want to ENCOURAGE you to
BELIEVE IN YOURSELF, to have
PRIDE in who you are and to find
COMFORT in your own skin,
to be CURIOUS about the world
around you, to DISCOVER
your voice, and to DREAM
as big as you can.

I want you to be confident in fighting for what you believe in, to be
ambitious about changing the world so it is fairer for everyone. I
want you to encourage others to use their voice too!

There are moments when these dreams might feel impossible. You might feel like giving up. You might feel like your dreams should belong to someone else. But, I'm here to remind you to have faith in yourself – because I've been in your shoes. I was a kid who felt different, I looked different to my friends and family, and at times, I was the kid who just wanted to fit in. But fitting in means hiding a part of yourself. It's choosing to not let the world see and experience all of who you are. I used to feel like hiding, but not any more. I've learned to be proud of who I am, to not be afraid of what others might think and to dream enormously big. And you can too.

I'd like to tell you something that I have learned:

THE IMPOSSIBLE *IS* POSSIBLE.

THE LIST OF DREAMS

From a young age, I kept a list of my dreams and ambitions. Throughout this book, you'll read some of my stories and the moments where so many of my dreams have come true. You'll learn about some of the people who have inspired me, and I'll introduce you to lots of amazing people you might not be taught about in school.

So, what's on your list? Because you might be different or feel different to the other people in your class or your family, but this book is here to help you find the power in being different, to discover the things you love about yourself, to grow your confidence, to follow your dreams, to break the mould and to find your place in the world.

Grab a pen and a piece of paper and start writing your list of dreams and ambitions. Remember, this is YOUR list, so write everything and anything on it that you want to achieve - even if it seems impossible. Especially, if it seems impossible!

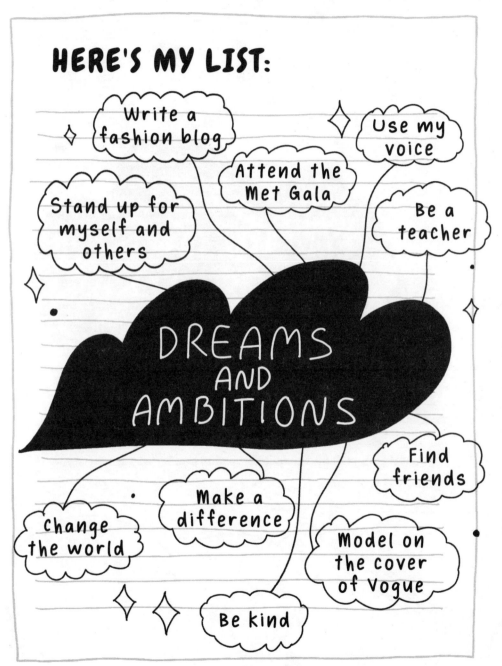

NOW IT'S YOUR TURN

Decorate your list and keep it somewhere safe, a place where you can refer to it often.

No one else has to see it if you don't want them to. Or you could share it with your family or friends and encourage them to write a list too.

It is up to YOU.
This is all about YOU.
It is the start of YOUR
BRILLIANT journey!

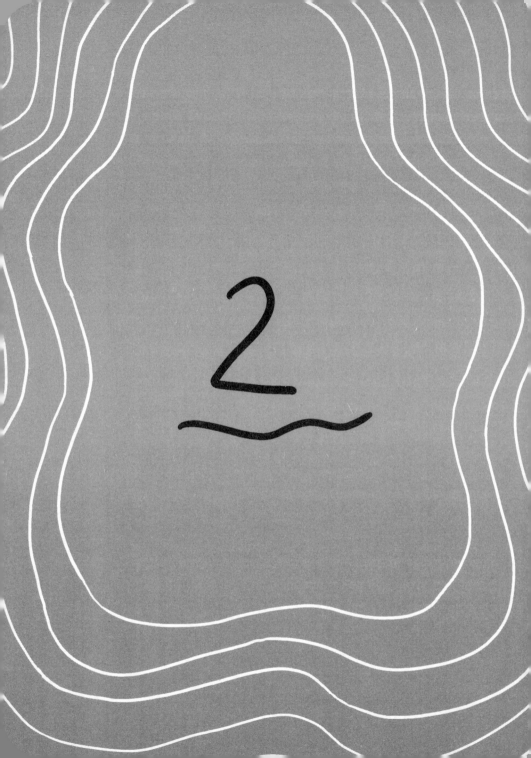

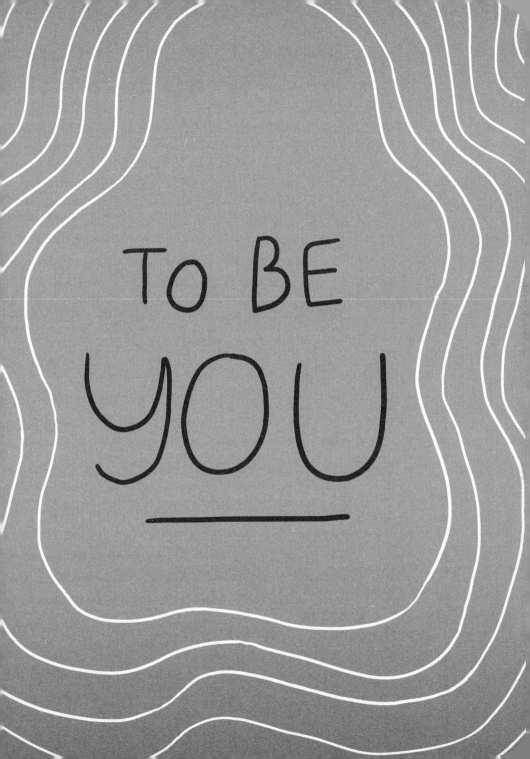

In the beginning, we don't get to choose who we are. In reality, so much of who we are is out of our control. When I was born, I didn't get to choose my name, the colour of my skin, the shape of my nose, if I was a boy or a girl, the type of family that I would be part of, the religion I would practise, the country I would be born in or where I would lay my head each night. You didn't either. Each of these characteristics and factors make us who we are as individuals, they form the basis of our identity, and shape how we behave and how we see the world. We inherit so much of what moulds us into ourselves.

But, what about if you had a **CHOICE**?
If you could **PICK AND CHOOSE**
the things that make you **YOU**?
What would you choose?

I experienced a taste of this once.

When I was in school, not only was I the smallest person in my class, but even as I got older, I was always the smallest person in my entire school. For class photographs, I would always sit in the front row, so that I could be seen. On Sports Day, my teacher would let me have a head start in many of the races. Yet, I would often forget that I was a little person, because looking through my eyes, I couldn't see what I looked like, even though it was so obvious to everyone else. I didn't realise I was small until I couldn't reach the light switch or I had to climb to wash my hands at the sink. Other times, I remembered that I was a little person because someone else pointed it out. That wasn't easy. In the playground at breaktime, I would spend time with my friends and there were times when someone from another class would come over and ask,

'WHY ARE YOU SO SMALL?'

or call me a hurtful name.

But I AM a little person. Because of my physical disability, my arms and legs are shorter than most people (sometimes known as average-height people). When I was eleven years old, I had an opportunity to change the way my body looked, and in turn, how others would see me. It was a big decision. The ability to change a part of myself was tempting and was possible with limb lengthening surgery that would make me taller.

Have you ever broken your arm or leg? Maybe you fell off your bike, tripped in gymnastics or dance class or just had an accident? It can happen almost too easily. After some panicked screams, you may have been brought to the hospital where the doctor held your broken bones very steadily, wrapped them in plaster of Paris and a brightly coloured cast. While your bones were in the cast, your limbs were quietly mending, growing back together and sealing the break to ensure that your arm or leg returned to being flexible and functional - almost like magic.

In many ways, the limb lengthening surgery was very similar to this. Instead of breaking a bone accidentally, my legs would have been deliberately fractured in the hospital by a doctor. Instead of giving me a cast for my bones to mend together, the doctors would have fitted a frame, called a fixator, to my limbs and tricked my bones into growing longer. It would take time but new bone would grow and I would be taller.

It would be complicated. It would be painful. School would be interrupted and I would use a wheelchair for several months, but I would be taller.

31

With the limb lengthening surgery, I might be able to do everything myself, without help. Maybe I would be able to reach the light switch. Maybe I wouldn't need the head start in the race on Sports Day and maybe other children wouldn't say cruel things in the playground. Maybe it would change my life, maybe my life would be a little easier. Maybe the pain would be worth it, because I would be taller.

Without the limb lengthening surgery, I would need help. I still wouldn't be able to reach the light switch. I would need the head start in the race on Sports Day and other children would probably still say cruel things in the playground. My life wouldn't change, but I would be me. Just me.

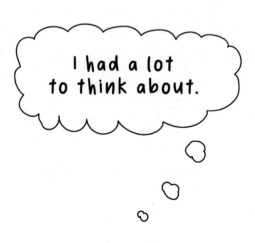

I had a lot to think about.

I made a list of the pros and cons.

On one side: light switch, Sports Day, playground. On the other side: being me.

Light switch

Sports Day

Playground

BEING ME

SO, WHY WOULD I
CHANGE WHO I AM?

At almost twelve years old, being able to reach things was important, but the most convincing reason for me choosing to make myself taller was that I would fit in more. I would look more like the other girls in my class and maybe I would make friends more easily. Maybe they would like me more, because the limb lengthening surgery would make me more like them.

After thinking about it a lot, I decided the surgery wasn't for me. That's not to say that limb lengthening surgery is wrong, just that it would have been wrong for me.

A LIFE-CHANGING DECISION

Perhaps you have already had to make a big decision to change something in your life, like I had to. Or perhaps you are thinking about something now, or you know someone who is deciding whether or not to make significant changes in their life.

It is hard and can be confusing.

Writing your thoughts down or talking with someone you trust can help make things clearer. But remember, if people only want to be your friend because you're willing to change who you are, they aren't the kind of people you want to call a friend. We deserve better friends,

friends who CELEBRATE and SUPPORT us and allow us to BE OURSELVES.

There are so many people in this world: 7.8 billion to be exact. But there is only one of me and one of you. We are all unique yet it's easy to think that we are not good enough, or maybe we spend too much time wishing that we could be more like our friends,

but the world would be DIFFERENT without YOU and ME.

Being a little person and being disabled has made me different, and it has also shaped me. It has moulded my personality. It has encouraged me to be kind. It has given me a perspective of the world that is unique. And it has allowed me to connect with people who feel a little bit different too.

I LOVE being me. I'm very PROUD to be ME.

THE THINGS THAT MAKE ME WHO I AM

There are no recipes for people, we are each made of different ingredients. These could be our race, gender, religion, disability, age, where we live, who we love and who loves us. Our differences may be visible, or they may be invisible. What makes us different might be obvious, or maybe it's not. But trust me, even if someone doesn't seem different, they are. Because, each one of us is different. I'm different, you're different. These differences give us a unique outlook on the world and a new way of seeing and experiencing things. These differences shape our personalities and mould our interests and dreams. This makes life interesting and unpredictable. If we were all made up from the same ingredients and recipes, if we were all the same, life would be quite boring and bland.

So, what makes you YOU? Being able to name the things that make you the person you are, and being able to understand why you see the world as you do and how the world sees you, marks the start of your journey to understanding how you can take your place in the world. A journey that will help you grow comfortable in your own skin and celebrate what makes you different. It will help you

discover your dreams and ambitions, and give you space to fulfil your potential. And as your confidence grows, you can start to use your voice to make a difference to those around you too.

But learning and discovering all of this takes time. So, if you don't know what makes you YOU just yet, don't worry … I'll go first.

I'm not always sure how to describe myself, there are lots of different things that make me who I am. I'm a daughter and a sister. I am a loving person who you call on your best and most challenging days. A person who will give you a hug on the days that you feel sad, and help you come up with a plan to feel better. A person who will take your side, but will tell you when you're not completely right.

I'm a loyal person. I'm a curious person. I'm a kind person. I'm a funny person. (Or, at least a person who tries to be funny!)

I love swimming, reading, fashion, talking to friends and travelling to new places. I love fizzy jellies, noodles and sushi, but not at the same time.

I love mint chocolate chip ice-cream and I am learning how to knit and how to grow plants.

My bed is an archive for things that matter to me. Under my pillow are objects that I treasure. At the end of my bed are notebooks, clothes that I promised I would hang up, and bits and pieces that I wanted to keep close to me. I collect items that remind me of lovely memories and I cherish birthday cards, letters and notes.

But, I'm not perfect. I'm a person who doesn't always get it right.

Like EVERYONE else, I make MISTAKES, but I try to LEARN from them.

My friends and family would probably say that I'm not a tidy person. I leave wet towels in places where they won't dry and I leave other things in places where only I can find them. Sometimes, even I'm not so good at finding the thing that I'm convinced I put somewhere safe. I overthink things and manage to make a small worry grow and grow. And I sometimes worry what people think of me, even though I know I shouldn't.

But I'm surrounded by brilliant people who are there for the good and the bad. They are clever, kind, funny, patient and loving. They give me space to discover who I am. They're my safety net and with them, I'm not afraid to take a leap and risk the fall. We should all try to surround ourselves with people who give us the confidence to try. But first things first, what makes you YOU ...

THE THINGS THAT MAKE YOU WHO YOU ARE

How would you describe yourself? What makes your heart race with excitement? What makes your mind fizz with ideas? What makes you feel proud of yourself? What makes you feel low?

What are you really good at?

What do you still need to work on?

What makes you different from me?

What makes you different from your friends?

43

Thinking about these things gives you an idea of the traits and characteristics that make you unique. It helps you to discover the things that you are proud of, and the things that you might not be so proud of and perhaps need to work on. It helps you work out who you are right now, and who you want to be in the future. No one is perfect. We are all a work in progress and our interests and ambitions might change, but getting to know who you are, understanding what makes you different and growing comfortable in who you are is the

first step to being able to take YOUR PLACE in the world.

Why not write a list of all the things that make you YOU? Then fold it up and put it somewhere safe. In a few months' time, seek it out, take a look and see which things have changed and what has stayed the same.

VOICES IN YOUR HEAD

Writing a list of the things that you are proud of and the things you still need to work on is not easy. It makes you feel a little vulnerable, and when I was writing my list, I spent quite a bit of time comparing myself to my brother, my sisters and my friends. I had to stop and remind myself that I was good enough, just as I was, even with my imperfections.

Have you ever felt sad or a bit low because you feel like you're not the smartest, the sportiest, the loudest, the most creative or the funniest person in your class? Do you compare yourself to other people and wish you were more like them?

Now, just for a second, imagine that the person you think is the smartest, the sportiest, the loudest, the most creative or the funniest person in class came up to you and said that they wish they were more like YOU. Yes, they think you're hilarious! Or really smart. Or amazingly sporty. Or brilliantly artistic. Or especially kind. Would you be surprised?

The truth is, we ALL spend time, too much time, comparing ourselves to others. We all have days where we don't feel good about ourselves and maybe, for just a minute, we wish that we could be someone else. But, it doesn't matter whether you're the most clever, the most athletic, the most vocal, the most artistic, or the most entertaining person. There are parts of your personality and identity that make you brilliant, unique and wonderful in your own way. It only matters that you are yourself.

So, next time that you hear that voice in your head doubting yourself, what will you say? And next time a friend says that they don't feel good enough, and they wish they could be someone else, what will you tell them? Look at your list to remind yourself of who you are, and how wonderfully unique you are, and then try saying some of these things out loud, to yourself or to your friends:

I AM GOOD ENOUGH /
YOU ARE GOOD ENOUGH.

I AM GREAT AT.../
YOU ARE GREAT AT...

I AM A GOOD FRIEND WHEN I.../
YOU ARE A GOOD FRIEND WHEN YOU...

I LIKE THAT I AM.../
I LIKE THAT YOU ARE...

I ALWAYS TRY.../
YOU ALWAYS TRY...

I AM PROUD OF.../
YOU ARE PROUD OF...

I AM ME. /
YOU ARE YOU.

I CAN BREAK THE MOULD. /
YOU CAN BREAK THE MOULD.

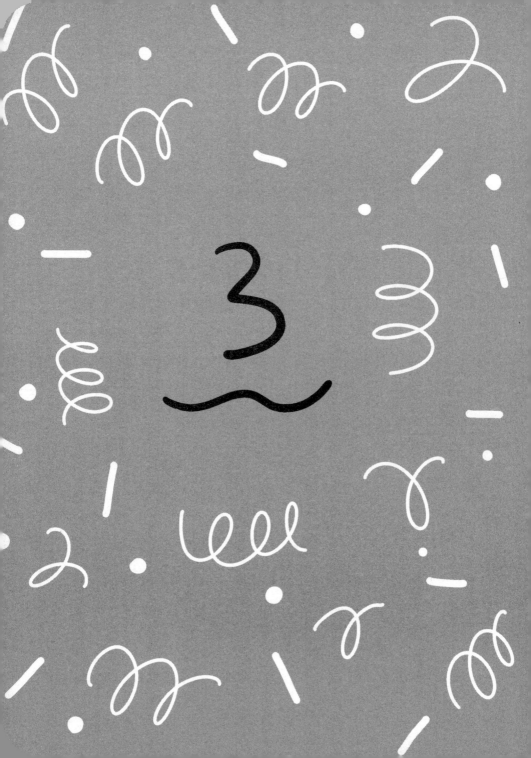

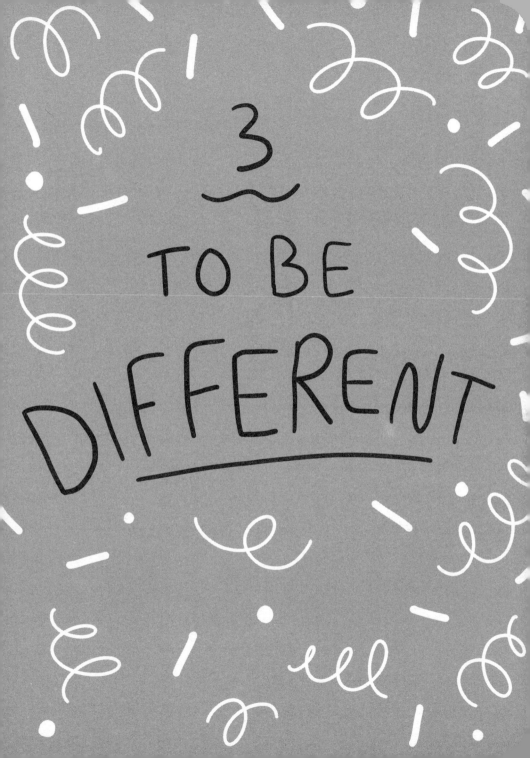

3

TO BE

DIFFERENT

What is it that makes us different? It can be the colour of our skin, the religion we practise, where we live, who we love, the languages we speak or having a disability. Whatever our difference, it shapes us - it moulds our personality, experience and skills.

Sometimes when I'm talking about my differences, I will say, 'I was just born like this,' which is true. Other times, I might also say that my difference is 'genetic'. But what does that mean?

Imagine that we are in a classroom - maybe it's your classroom - and I've asked for a volunteer. It's one of your classmates and they come up to the top of the room and stand beside me. Standing side by side, it's pretty obvious that they're bigger than me - by quite a bit. But when we sit down, on the same-sized chairs, I am taller. Why is that? How could I go from being smaller, to then being taller?

The answer is in my genes. We are all made of lots of different genes (around 20,000 in fact!). They make up who we are and what we look like. For me, one of my genes means that my arms and legs are smaller, so when I stand, I stand smaller than most children, but when I sit, I sit taller because my torso, which is from my shoulders to my hips, is taller.

Every single one of us has genes that make us who we are. Maybe you're the tallest person in your class, or the smallest person in your family. Maybe you have dark hair, or bright-coloured eyes.

Our mix of genes is UNIQUE to us and they set the foundation for who WE ARE.

We don't get to choose them; so much of what we look like, and who we are, is decided for us. But there are many parts of our personality that we can still choose ourselves.

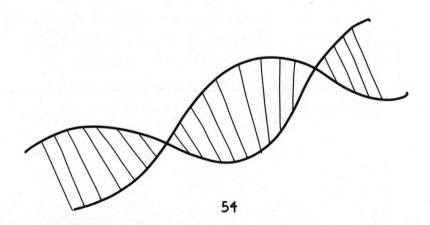

WHAT ARE GENES?

Humans are made up of billions of microscopic parts called cells. These cells contain DNA (deoxyribonucleic acid). Genes are a small section of this DNA and they work like instruction manuals telling your body what to do. They contain instructions that tell your cells how to make proteins – which help keep your body working and healthy. But genes also carry instructions that determine your features, like whether you have straight or curly hair, or what colour eyes you have. Sometimes genes are inherited so that traits are passed from one family member to another. This means you might have the same eye colour or blood type as your parent.

Being a little person was in my genes, and it has shaped my personality and skills. I am organised, creative and articulate - not in spite of my disability, but because of it. I'm organised and creative because I'm constantly planning and thinking, knowing that it might take me longer to do something, or I might have to figure out a different way altogether. And, I'm articulate because I use words to communicate to the world who I am, I use my voice to create change and to educate others on how to think about difference and disability.

CREATE CHANGE!

Our **DIFFERENCES** can guide us to **UNDERSTAND** the world, and other people too.

There are so many people who are different, just like you and me. Their difference has shaped their dreams and ambitions, and all that they have achieved. Let me introduce you to them.

YASH GUPTA has worn glasses since he was five years old, but one day during Taekwondo practice, he broke them. He didn't realise how much he needed them until everything was a blur. It made him question how many other children needed glasses too. He learned that throughout the world, there are 12 million children who do not have the glasses that they need. Their vision is constantly a blur. At fourteen, Yash wanted to help and wanted to make a difference. He began by gathering up all the old pairs of glasses he had at home. Then he visited his local opticians and asked them if he could have the spare glasses they were no longer using. He donated them to charities and organisations that could give the glasses to the children who needed them. Since then, Yash has collected and donated more than 60,000 pairs of glasses.

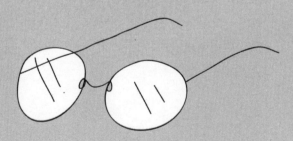

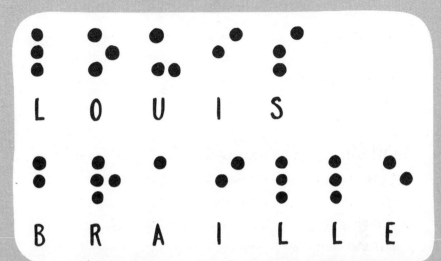

LOUIS

BRAILLE

was born over two hundred years ago, in the 19th century. He became blind at five years old and went to one of the first schools for blind children in Paris. In his early teenage years, he learned that the army were using a language of dots and lines to communicate privately with one another. The dots and lines were carved into thick paper and by running your fingertips across them, were easily felt. The army's system was complicated, so Louis simplified it using six dots organised in 63 different ways to create a new language for blind people to communicate. Louis named this language after himself and called it Braille. This language is still being used today.

MARLEY DIAS was just eleven years old when she realised that the characters in the books she was reading did not look like her – they were nearly always white children. Occasionally, there would be a Black girl or boy, but they were background characters and rarely spoke. Marley wanted this to change. She began a campaign, a project that could make a difference. She created a hashtag, which is a way for people to find a conversation online and get involved too. Marley's campaign was called #1000BlackGirlBooks and her dream was to find and collect one thousand books where the main characters were young Black girls, just like her. In a very short time, she collected over nine thousand books and proved to the world that stories are important and we all deserve to pick up a book and see ourselves in it.

WHAT ABOUT YOU?

Thinking of Yash, Louis and Marley, they each have different identities. Identities shaped by genetics, by culture and by where and how they live. Their identities have shaped their personality, skills and dreams. What makes them different is what makes them unique. But they have also used their experiences to make a real difference to the world around them.

For Yash, wearing glasses helps him to see. He didn't realise how important his glasses were to him until they broke and his vision was blurred. It made him question if he was alone, if he was the only person who wears glasses. He learned that lots of people need to wear glasses, but not everyone can access or afford them. Knowing how important they were to him, Yash found, collected and donated glasses so that thousands of other children could see the world as clearly as him. Without Yash's difference, he would probably never have created this project and changed the world.

We are all different and these experiences shape our personalities, skills and dreams in unique and brilliant ways. But, what makes you different and unique?

Take a second to think about your differences, and how they have shaped you. Maybe you are sensitive but those sensitivities mean that you might be able to help your friends or a brother or a sister when they are upset. You may know what to say to give them comfort and to help them feel better.

You could use your list of the things that make you YOU to guide you. Is it the way you look? The way you walk? The language you speak or how you talk? Is it your culture or religion? Is it your wheelchair or your hearing aid? Or is it something invisible - something that people can't see?

Noting what makes you different, being proud and celebrating who you are is brave and important, but not always easy. There are times when we might feel like we are alone, that we don't belong and we don't have a place in the world. But I promise you, the things that make you unique can be a very powerful tool and, when you realise this, the world is yours and you can dream and achieve the impossible.

You are ENOUGH as you are. You don't need to CHANGE to make a DIFFERENCE, but EMBRACING what makes you DIFFERENT can create a CHANGE.

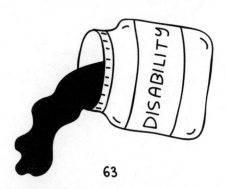

There is no one way to use your difference to break the mould and create change, but to help you find your way, here is a list of things that have helped me - five steps for identifying your differences and using your voice to take your place in the world.

MY TIPS FOR EMBRACING YOUR DIFFERENCE AND MAKING YOUR MARK

① Accept Yourself, Warts and All!

Growing comfortable with who you are and learning to recognise what makes you different, unique and interesting takes time. There are parts of yourself that you might love, like or hide. But all of those things should be symbols of pride, not embarrassment, and feeling proud of them will encourage other people to celebrate those parts too! Learning to accept yourself will not only help to make your dreams and ambitions a reality, but it will give others the courage and confidence to do that too.

Remember those important lists you made – about your dreams and ambitions, about the qualities and factors that make you who you are, and the things you can say to make you feel proud of who you are? Take a look at them now, and whenever you need a little extra help accepting yourself, warts and all.

② Be Curious

Have you ever wondered how you're different to the other people in your class? Or wondered about how they seem different to you? Or have you thought about why we do things in a certain way? Learning about the world, different perspectives and new ideas has never been easier, or more important.

UNDERSTANDING people from different BACKGROUNDS, experiences and BELIEFS will make the world a better place, and you a BETTER PERSON.

You can do this by asking questions, as long as they are kind and appropriate. You can also read books or watch films where the characters look different to you, so that you can learn about their experiences and ways of life. And if people ask you about your experiences, share stories about parts of your life, culture, beliefs or genetic make-up that make you proud of who you are.

③ Find Your People

When I was seven years old, my parents founded Little People of Ireland; an organisation for little people and their families. The idea was to create a community for people who share a common bond to come together, to share advice, and to make life-long friends with people who understand your experiences. It was one of the moments that changed me because all of a sudden, there were other children who looked like me and families who were like my family. No matter what your experience, try to find people who you trust - friends, parents, a grandparent, a brother or a sister, people who will support you and celebrate you as you race towards your goals!

Note: Finding friends is important and sometimes you might have one friend, four friends or a whole group of friends. It doesn't matter how many friends you have, but it's the kind of friend that they are that's important. Don't settle for the people who don't make you feel good about yourself, who say and do cruel things, maybe to be cool or popular. They're not true friends. Find the people who make you happy, and you can do that for them too!

④ Be Kind to You

It's important to always remember to be kind to yourself. We all have that voice in our heads, that sometimes whispers that we are not good enough, that we shouldn't try, that our dreams are for someone else to achieve and that we should just give up. But, that voice doesn't speak the truth. That voice is our fears and our nerves coming to life. So, be kind to you. Turn that voice off, lower the volume and don't listen to it. Instead, programme the voice in your head to say:

'You are good enough! You need to give this a try! You are the best person to do this! Your **DREAMS** are so close, they're almost a reality! **NEVER GIVE UP!'**

⑤ Don't Settle for the Status Quo

If someone tells you that something is impossible, or it cannot be done, ask them why. The status quo is a way of describing the way that the world currently works. But this can, and should, change and you have the ability and opportunity to do that.

THE IMPOSSIBLE ONLY SEEMS IMPOSSIBLE BECAUSE IT HASN'T HAPPENED BEFORE. YOU CAN MAKE A DIFFERENCE AND MAKE A CHANGE.

It takes time to accept yourself, just as you are. There will be days when you feel invincible, and others where you wish that you could be like everyone else. But being different is part of you, it's part of me, it's part of being us and there is no one quite like you and me. Allow these five tips to be your guide, to remind yourself, whenever you need a boost.

UNSUNG HEROES: THE PEOPLE YOU'RE NOT TAUGHT ABOUT AT SCHOOL

JUDY HEUMANN is an American disability rights activist. When she was a child, Judy wanted to be a teacher but was told that her dream was impossible because she uses a wheelchair. Judy knew that this was wrong and unfair, she fought this rule in court and became the first teacher who was a wheelchair user in New York City.

Judy has spent her life working to make the world a fairer place – especially for disabled people. Once, she even protested against the US government by sitting in their offices and refusing to leave for 25 days until the law was changed and the rights of disabled people were protected.

Recently, Judy was an advisor to President Barack Obama in the White House and was the first disability advisor at the World Bank.

The FIRST
teacher who was a wheelchair user in New York City

WE ARE ALL DIFFERENT, BUT WE ARE THE SAME

Now that you have my tips for making your mark, and you've discovered the importance of accepting who you are and what makes you different, let's spend a moment thinking about the people around us - in our home, in our school and in our community.

Have you noticed that everyone is different? Look around.

Whether it's our skin colour, age, disability, religion, family make-up, who we love or where we live, we are all different. These differences make life rich, exciting and interesting. They allow us to have important friendships and to learn about new ways of experiencing and seeing the world.

But, look closely. Do you notice anything that joins all of these people together?

Quite a few people have blue eyes, more have brown hair and almost everyone has a nose, because even though we are all different, in ways that are visible and invisible, we are all people.

We all have
FEARS, WORRIES,
ANXIETIES,
HOPES and
DREAMS

We all want to have friends, and to feel connected, but at times what makes us different can make us feel alone. We feel like we are the only who who is just like us. We are! That's true! But it's something to be proud of and to celebrate. There really is only one of me and one of you. We matter.

We are all different. Which, in a way, makes us all the same because those differences are what bring us together. We all experience the world from a unique perspective. We are all humans that have more in common than you might think. There is more that connects us than divides us.

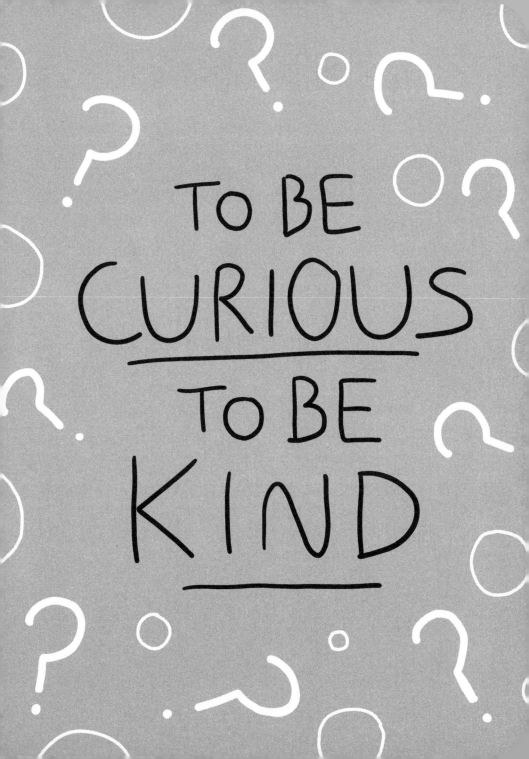

There's a feeling you sometimes get. It starts at the base of your spine and slowly it rolls towards your neck. It peels upwards, vertebrae by vertebrae, and feels so real that you could touch it, or swat it away. Before lifting your head, or turning around, you know what will meet your eye. Someone is staring. At you.

We've all experienced an awkward moment like this, maybe in school or on the bus. You have drifted off into a daydream and haven't registered that someone is talking to you. It isn't until you feel yourself being stared at that you suddenly awaken from your daydream, flushed with embarrassment.

You feel uncomfortable because someone else has made you the centre of attention, even though you didn't ask to be. I've been there! Knowing that people are looking at me and staring at me is something that I have always lived with. I am often the centre of attention - but usually not by choice.

I look different to most people. It's possible that if we meet, I could be the first little person that you have ever seen. It's possible that you would have questions and might want to know how and why I am a little person, and what those words mean.

Curiosity is natural but being openly curious can take bravery. Asking questions reveals what we don't know, but it can be difficult to find the right words because we don't want to say or do the wrong thing. It can make us vulnerable and it can dissolve some of our confidence. But asking questions to learn about the world from a new perspective has never been more important.

It's likely that many of us have also experienced other people asking us questions - people who notice our differences and want to learn more. So, we need to think about two things. The first,

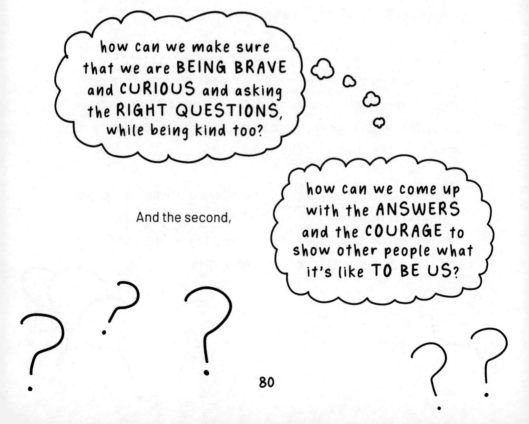

how can we make sure that we are BEING BRAVE and CURIOUS and asking the RIGHT QUESTIONS, while being kind too?

And the second,

how can we come up with the ANSWERS and the COURAGE to show other people what it's like TO BE US?

WHY DON'T YOU SAY HELLO?

I could be in a supermarket, and a child, probably someone younger than you, will see me. They're not sure if I am an adult or a child, but from a very young age, they can tell that something is different about me. They get excited and want to make sure that whoever is with them has seen me too. To the entire aisle, and other shoppers too, they announce, 'Look, there's a little woman'.

For the next few minutes, it's as if everything moves in slow motion.

That feeling of being stared at begins; my shoulders rise to my ears and I'm uncomfortable. But maybe not for the reason you think. I'm not angry or upset with them, I'm just a little cautious about what might happen next.

Usually it goes something like this: the adult tries to create a distraction. They show them some groceries that are on the shelves, maybe some sweets, but in an even louder voice, the child says, 'No. Look! There's a little woman. Right there!'

The adult is embarrassed. They're trying hard not to hurt my feelings and they don't know what to say, or how to say it. So, they choose to say nothing at all.

Moving from slow motion to fast forward; the trolley zips past me, racing to the next aisle as fast as possible, with the child desperately clinging to the sides.

I know the adult was trying to help. They thought that they were doing the right thing, but they were uncomfortable and embarrassed. They didn't have the words or know how to explain to the child that I'm a little person.

Maybe you've experienced something like this. Perhaps you saw someone who looked different to you in the playground or the school yard. You wanted to talk to them, ask them a question and learn about their differences, but you didn't know how. You didn't want to say the wrong thing or upset them.

But it's okay to ask questions. Curiosity is great and asking questions can help you to understand the world through a new lens. It can help others feel more comfortable too. If something interests you or you want to know something, asking a question is a good thing.

When I was teaching in the classroom, moments like this would happen - particularly on the first day of school. My students would come into the classroom and I would begin to introduce myself. I remember one time, I hadn't even finished mentioning my name when in the corner of my eye, I could see a girl waving her hand in the air. She was leaning out of her seat and concentrating so hard on the question she wanted to ask, that I'm not sure if she remembered to breathe. I called her name and said, 'Yes?'

'WHY ARE YOU SO SMALL?'

The children who sat closest to my desk gasped and looked at each other.

'WHY ARE YOU SO BIG?'

I asked her.

83

I could tell from her facial expression that she wasn't sure why.

'I DON'T KNOW, I WAS JUST BORN LIKE THIS,'

she said.

I responded with a grin and said,

'ME TOO.'

It was so simple, but it made sense. I didn't choose my disability or the body that I live within, but neither did she. Though the conversation might have been a little awkward at first, by explaining my difference in this way, we all realised that much of our experience is universal. As we now know, what makes us different is sometimes what makes us the same. We are all

people. We all need food and sleep. We all want to be loved. We all have moments when we think that we are not good enough.

Someone might ask you a question about what makes you different and if it makes you feel uncomfortable, it is okay to say, 'I would prefer not to talk about that.' But if you think the person is asking because they are curious and want to learn about what it's like to be you, let them know that, just like them, you were born this way. It answers their question and helps them to realise that it's not just you or me who is different, they're different too.

These conversations can be awkward. We don't want to upset anyone, or say the wrong thing, but if we did nothing, and didn't speak to people who look, sound and think differently to us, because of fear, nervousness or embarrassment, we'd have no idea of who or what things we were missing out on.

Being <u>CURIOUS</u> about our <u>DIFFERENCES</u> makes us realise that being different isn't a bad thing, it brings us together and connects us.

That moment in the supermarket could have been a positive experience for everyone with just one simple phrase. When the child pointed me out, the adult could have said,

'YES, THAT IS A LITTLE WOMAN – WHY DON'T YOU SAY HELLO?'

Can you imagine what would have happened next? I bet the kid would have waved, said hello and told me their name. They would have said it proudly and loudly. I would have waved and said that my name is Sinéad.

We'd both smile and continue with our shopping trip.

JACINDA ARDERN is the Prime Minister of New Zealand, which means that she leads the government and is responsible for making many of the decisions for her country. When she was elected, she was the youngest female head of government and only the second woman ever to have a baby while in that position.

When you can't see yourself represented, it's easy to think the job is not for you, or there's only one way to do it. Jacinda didn't try to be other people, she was comfortable in her own skin and is a leader who is praised for leading in a new way, for leading with kindness, empathy and compassion.

Can you remember any moments where you wished that you had talked to someone, asked a question, but didn't know what to say? Out of fear and embarrassment, you said nothing. It might seem easier, but by allowing that fear and embarrassment to take hold, we are stopping ourselves from meeting and learning about people who will make our lives and world more interesting .

Next time, use your voice. Speak to a child who is different to you - in the yard, or the playground - you'll learn something about them and something about you too. You might even make a friend.

THE CENTRE OF ATTENTION

Having honest and even awkward conversations is a good thing. But, not all curiosity is kind. There are times when you may be stared at, laughed at, pointed out or even made to feel unimportant or worthless. The reasons why make no sense at all.

There are times when I've been walking towards a group of people and laughter erupts. They think it's okay to laugh at me because, being a little person, I'm in a minority. You might be in a minority because of your gender, race, religion, disability, language or your family make-up. You might be the only one like you in your class or in the playground. We're all different, but being in a minority can bring an added challenge.

I have been called names and words that make me shrink inside myself, and sometimes photographs are taken of me without my permission. Why, might you ask? I ask myself the same thing.

There was even a time when a stranger took a photo of me from their car. I was walking and noticed that a car had slowed to my pace, right beside me. They lowered the window, took a photo and drove off.

DISABILITY

My body rattled. I got a fright, I was upset and couldn't stop crying. They didn't know who I was, nor did they care. I was just something for them to laugh at, they didn't think of me as a person. I was afraid, and so hurt by their cruelty. I couldn't understand why they would act and behave like this. I did nothing wrong. I was just being myself.

Each time someone stared at me, or pointed me out, it was a reminder that I am different. This could have made me think that my difference wasn't to be celebrated and maybe even something that I should try to hide from, but my family taught me differently.

My family doesn't look like most families, but there are many families like mine. My dad is a little person and my mam is average height. I am the eldest of five children; I have three sisters and one brother, and I'm the only one of the children who is a little person.

I wasn't always comfortable with being the centre of attention, or with answering strangers' questions, but I've learned how to manage it and to see each awkward conversation as a bridge closer to living in a world that encourages every person to just be themselves. I've learned that being different is worth celebrating.

I remember chatting with my parents about what makes people do and say things that are hurtful and unkind. Why do people think it's okay to instil fear in others and make them feel less? We didn't have all of the answers to these big questions but talking it through helped. My parents reminded me I can't control how other people behave towards me, it's not my fault and it's not my responsibility.

'WHO DO YOU WANT
TO BE, SINÉAD?'

they asked.

'Do you want to be a person who chooses to make others cry, to make them feel less, in order to make yourself feel better?

Or ...

93

DO YOU WANT TO BE
A PERSON WHO <u>LIGHTS</u>
<u>A ROOM</u>, AND MAKES OTHER
PEOPLE FEEL BETTER
ABOUT THEMSELVES, SIMPLY
BY <u>BEING YOU?</u>'

I still think of this conversation today, because I choose to be a kind person. I choose to make people feel better about themselves and the world after having a conversation with me. I choose to answer people's curious questions and teach them about life as a little person. I choose to be kind to people, my friends, my family and myself. I choose to proudly take my place in the world.

GLAD TO BE ME

Throughout your life, some people may choose to be mean. They might try to convince you to not be proud of yourself and to think of your difference as something that should make you feel less. But if this happens, remember that their actions and words do not define you, that they don't have the power to shape who you are, so you shouldn't let this shape how you feel about yourself.

There are three things that I do to help remind myself that I am glad to be me. Why don't you try them too?

1. I remind myself that there is only ONE of me, that I am SMART, KIND and sometimes FUNNY.

2. I remind myself that I am PROUD OF WHO I AM, and I CELEBRATE what makes me DIFFERENT.

3. I remind myself that I am a GOOD FRIEND, a person who HELPS others see the value in being themselves.

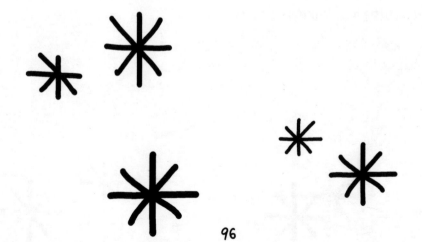

We all have the power to make our friends and the people we meet feel confident to be themselves too. So why not start now? You could ask a friend about the things you have always admired about them, and get them to tell you more about how it feels to be them. This will help them realise they are also unique and special, and you might even discover something you didn't know about them too. You could even ask these questions to someone you haven't spoken to much before.

But I know these conversations can be difficult and maybe you don't feel ready to have them yet. That's okay! Why not start with a simple 'Hello, what's your name?'

It's just a small step, but people won't forget the effort you've made.

TO FIND
YOUR
WORDS

Choosing the right words at the right time can be difficult. Knowing what to say and how to say it takes practice. But language and words are important. They are the tools we use to communicate, to tell the world who we are and to learn about other experiences. Words can bring you down or they can lift you up. Just think of a time when someone has said something nasty to you and how that has made you feel. Then compare it with the way you have felt when someone has said something lovely to you! Words are powerful.

Language is constantly changing too. It evolves over time and morphs depending on who is saying it, when they are saying it and why are they saying it. That sounds confusing, but you change your language and vocabulary all of the time - maybe without even realising it! When you talk to a friend, because you know each other so well, the language you use is more casual, you have your own short-hand way of saying things. You may even finish each other's sentences or you can predict what the other person is going to say! In school, when you talk to your teacher, you're more formal - you might pronounce every letter and syllable accurately and pay close attention to the words you choose.

You might also change your language at home. Maybe in school you speak English and at home you speak Spanish, or French, or Irish, or Arabic, or Swahili or Urdu. Or maybe you communicate with your hands, signing and lip-reading words. There are many ways we can express ourselves and connect with the people around us.

LANGUAGE I LOVE

What are your favourite words? Define each word and share them with your friends or family, explaining what they mean.

Here are a few of my favourite words: **AMELIORATE, CANTANKEROUS, EMPATHY, MÉLANGE** and **INEFFABLE**. I like the action of pronouncing them and learning the ways in which my face has to shift and change to say them correctly.

(By the way, in case you were wondering what they mean, or how you say them, here are some definitions ...)

AMELIORATE
(A-MEE-LEE-OR-ATE)

A verb that means to make something better.

CANTANKEROUS
(CAN-TANK-OR-US)

An adjective that describes someone who is argumentative and unhelpful.

EMPATHY
(EM-PAH-TH-EE)

A noun that means to understand and share someone else's feelings and experiences.

INEFFABLE
(IN-EF-A-BULL)

An adjective that means something that is so incredible you can barely find the words to explain it.

MÉLANGE
(MAY-LAWN-J):

A noun that describes a mixture.

LANGUAGE IS A POWERFUL TOOL

Have you ever looked at the objects and the people that surround you and wondered how they got their names?

Language is a powerful tool. It doesn't just name our world, it shapes it.

But our relationship with language can be a little complicated. Mine is. Maybe you have been called names that upset you? Words that hurt because of the colour of your skin, your disability, your gender or your religion, your age, for who you love and who loves you, or for another reason ... or for no real reason at all.

But sometimes, it's not even about the words that other people call you, but the words you use to describe yourself.

When I was younger, I didn't want to give myself a label. It made me feel even more different to my friends, and all I wanted to be was Sinéad.

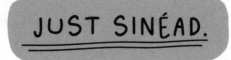

JUST SINÉAD.

I guess in a way, maybe I thought that having a label was something to be embarrassed about or ashamed of. I was keen to look, think and feel like everyone else, and my words mirrored these fears and anxieties.

I'M DISABLED. I AM VERY **PROUD** TO BE DISABLED.

Yet, when some people hear that word, they become awkward and not sure how to speak to or act towards me. I think it's because in the past, when we described someone as disabled, it meant that there was something wrong with them. A divide was created between non-disabled people and disabled people. It was an old way of thinking that came from fear and nervousness.

I became an advocate, which is a person who believes in something and tries to make a difference, and my thinking changed. I began to understand and accept that my difference and my disability was something to be proud of. I began to allow myself to use the word disabled and proudly spoke about the many ways that I was different. It was a badge of honour. After all, being a little person had shaped my personality and allowed me to become a person that I loved, admired and respected. It allowed me to be me!

Language is personal and powerful. It has the potential to make people feel included, accepted and lifted. But it can also cause upset, harm and hurt.

Knowing which words to use and when to use them is not always easy. Particularly when there isn't one agreed term - not everyone chooses to use the same words or the same language to describe themselves. For me, I am most comfortable with being described as a little person, but others might prefer words such as dwarf, person with restricted growth or person of short stature. The words that make one person comfortable, might make another uncomfortable.

Maybe think of it like this: if someone called 'Kimberly' told you that they didn't like being called 'Kim', then it wouldn't be very kind to go around calling them Kim, would it? And to people who aren't called Kimberly or Kim, they might not think it's a big deal ... why should it matter, they're both just names?! But you don't know what feelings a certain name can summon for someone, so it's always better to be curious and to ask to make sure you aren't going to hurt anyone's feelings.

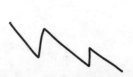

WHAT SHOULD I CALL YOU?

To help figure out how to do that, here's a story of when I was at school. I was much younger than you and one of the girls in my class asked me a question.

'WHAT SHOULD I CALL YOU?' they said.

I was confused. 'What do you mean?'

'BECAUSE YOU'RE SMALL, BECAUSE YOU'RE DIFFERENT. WHAT'S THE WORD?'

'I'm a little person,' I said proudly.

'But, my name is Sinéad. You can call me Sinéad.'

Everyone will have words, names and labels that they like and dislike, and sometimes you might feel too shy to ask. If that's the case, and if you're ever in doubt, the best thing to call someone is by their name!

INVENTING NEW WORDS

But what about if the words that you're comfortable with don't exist? The amazing thing about language is that it's constantly changing and evolving. Each year, over 1,000 words are added to the dictionary and some words and meanings have changed completely over time.

Did you know that *'nice'* once meant silly, foolish and simple?

Or that **'naughty'** used to mean evil, rather than just badly behaved?

Or that **'clue'** was understood to be a ball of wool?

Or that **'FUDGE'** meant lies and nonsense, that it was something you said, not something you ate?

I speak a few different languages: English, Irish and French. I love the Irish language but when I was at school, there was no word for little person in the Irish dictionary. There was a word for dwarf, but I needed language that would give me confidence and that I could be comfortable with.

I thought to myself,

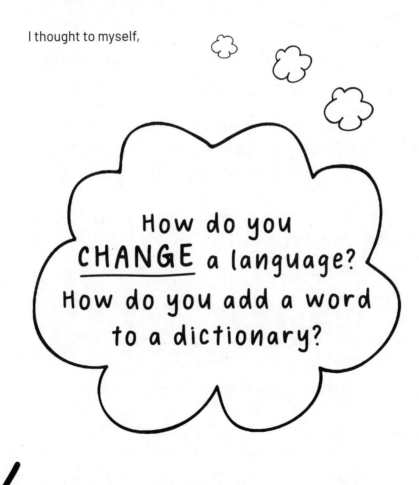

How do you **CHANGE** a language? How do you add a word to a dictionary?

I did some research and learned that Fóras na Gaeilge is the organisation that oversees the development of the Irish language. I got in touch with them and said, 'Hi, my name is Sinéad Burke; I'm a teacher and a little person. Unfortunately, there is no word in the Irish language that allows me to say this sentence in *Gaeilge*. How can we add the term little person to the dictionary?'

I didn't think that they would reply. But they did, and really quickly too.

'Hi Sinéad, you're right, it doesn't exist but this sounds like a great idea. Do you have any suggestions for what the new word could be?'

'Sure,' I replied. 'What about the direct translation of 'little person'? *Duine beag*.'

TO SAY DUINE BEAG, IT SOUNDS LIKE THIS:
DIN - A - BE - YUGG

'That's perfect. We'll add it to the dictionary right now.'

And they did!

DUINE BEAG
(din - a - be - yugg)

Little person

In just three days, I added a new term to the Irish dictionary and it was made official. I changed the Irish language! Now people had a more sensitive and appropriate term they could officially use.

Language and words are malleable, which means that they're flexible and can change over time and with other people's input. Are there any words that you think should be invented? Funny words that will bring people joy? Kind words that will make people happy? Or empowering words that will bring people confidence? Are there any words that you believe we should remove? Words that make people uncomfortable or are a little outdated?

WHEN CHANGE ISN'T ALWAYS POSITIVE

Sometimes, the way language is used isn't always positive. There are lots of words that can sometimes mean the same thing or similar things, and using the wrong one might cause upset. The language that I use to describe myself is often different to the words that I hear muttered as I walk past a group of strangers, or if someone is trying to make fun of me. Sometimes they use a word that's really hurtful - they call me a 'midget'.

When I hear it, I stop. I become aware of the quickening of my breath and my pulse. I can feel my temperature increase, and I start to sweat. I panic. When people use that word, it makes me feel unsafe, uncomfortable and it is used to remind me that I am different to them - a difference that is not to be celebrated but one that is supposed to make me feel less of a person.

The word midget is an old and out-of-date term. It first came into circulation almost two hundred years ago, but became popular thanks to one man, P.T. Barnum. He was famous for gathering people who were different and bringing them together in a circus for audiences to observe and spectate. It was a long time ago, when the world was less accepting of people who looked like me. There were few jobs and opportunities to go to school, so what P.T. was offering, I imagine, was very tempting.

To introduce the audience to people who looked like me, P.T. Barnum would describe them as midgets. At every show he was creating an awareness of this word, but at the time, it didn't cause the upset it causes today.

The world has changed. Little people are educated and diverse and work in many professions. Just like the average-height community, many little people choose to work in areas such as education, healthcare, hospitality, entertainment, manufacturing and many more. The possibility of what we can achieve and accomplish is almost limitless.

Yet, still, the word 'midget' is used. This must change. We must choose to use language and words that are kind, that reflect our reality, and most importantly, give people permission to feel proud of who they are. But, how do we change it?

You can.

There are lots of words that are no longer appropriate or kind. You might know of a few. You might have been called them or used them yourself without realising how hurtful they are.

It takes practice to learn new ways of saying old things. You might make a mistake, or say an old word accidentally or unintentionally. The important thing is that you try; over time, choosing to use kind words will become completely natural.

You have the power to make a difference and you can also teach your friends and family new, kinder words. If they make a mistake, you can say, 'Hey, that word isn't cool.'

AWKWARD....

This all might sound easy, but sometimes when someone says or does something that is uncool, it can feel too awkward to say anything. We might end up feeling embarrassed or reluctant to make a fuss. Over time I've been collecting and creating phrases and sentences that I use when people say something that's no longer acceptable (or has never been acceptable). I hope they might help you navigate awkward and uncomfortable situations with confidence and style!

TOP TIPS FOR AWKWARD SITUATIONS

Situation (1) If someone is trying to be kind, but they're using words that are outdated, and language that I don't identify with, I try to remind them of other words that they could use instead. For example, if they have described me as a dwarf, and not a little person, I might say something like:

'I **understand** that you might not know, and that you are trying to be sensitive with the words that you use, but I don't describe myself as a dwarf. Some other people do, but I **choose** to describe myself as a little person. **In future,** when you are talking about and to me, could you use little person, or my name, Sinéad?'

This script isn't just for little people, it's for anybody who is different. If you would like others to describe you with language that makes you comfortable, change 'dwarf', 'little person' and 'Sinéad' to the words that fit your experience, your identity and the things that make you different.

Situation ② If someone is trying to hurt your feelings, or if they're trying to hurt your friend, or your brother or sister, you might try to help by reminding them of **other words** that they could use instead. But, you could also tell an adult, a parent, a teacher, or someone who can help. When I was a teacher, one of my students once came to me and said:

'A boy was in the yard at lunchtime and one of the older boys, for **no reason at all,** started to call him names, they hit him and they made him very upset. I didn't know what to do, I didn't feel safe telling them to stop, but I wanted to do something. I wanted to help.'

This is a brave thing to do. Telling someone you trust will make you feel better and help you understand that what happened wasn't your fault. But it also means that the parent, teacher, or older friend can then talk to the people causing the problem and teach them about the impact of their actions, the ways in which we are all different and the importance of being respectful and kind.

Thinking about words and using our voices to tell the world who we are proud to be and how we feel has never been more important. Even though it's not easy, and it takes practice, it's not impossible.

SPEAK MY LANGUAGE

There are over six thousand spoken languages in the world, but some languages are not heard, they're seen. Sign language is made up of facial expressions, hand movements and symbols, used mostly by Deaf people. The movements convey more than just a sound – they also express ideas and feelings.

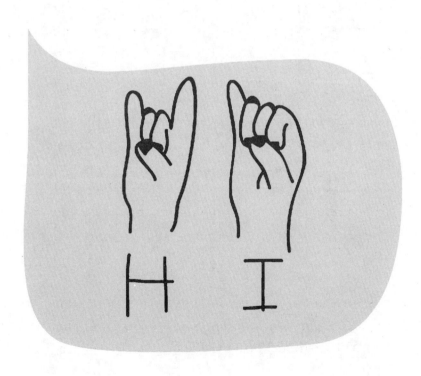

Just as different countries around the world have different spoken languages, they also have different sign languages. If we look at the Irish Sign Language (ISL) and the British Sign Language (BSL) we can see some of their differences. The Irish manual sign alphabet uses one hand for finger spelling,

ISL

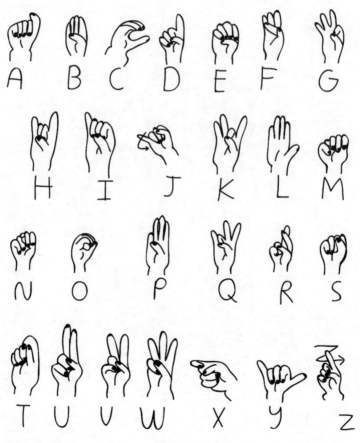

whereas the British manual sign alphabet uses two hands. Take a look at both their alphabets. Try signing your name in both ISL and BSL. And if you don't know sign language already, why not learn to say, 'Hi, how are you?' so you can communicate with someone whose first language is ISL or BSL?

BSL

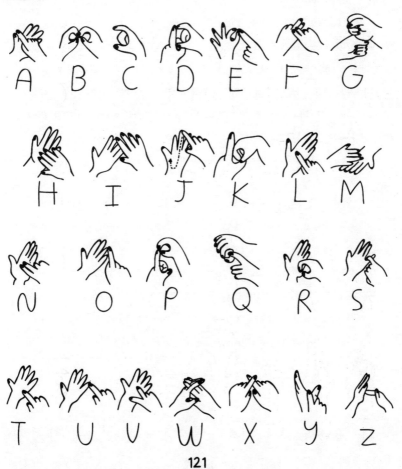

UNSUNG HEROES: THE PEOPLE YOU'RE NOT TAUGHT ABOUT AT SCHOOL

CHRISTINE SUN KIM *is a Deaf artist and activist who believes in the power of art to communicate between those who hear, and those who are Deaf. Describing the differences between spoken languages and American Sign Language, Christine thinks of music and playing the piano. She suggests that the English language is like playing one note at a time, we use words as building blocks to create sentences. But sign language is like a chord, you press ten fingers into the keys all at once to create not just one sound, but an idea and a feeling.*

Christine does not use her literal voice to communicate, but she is not voiceless. She is a powerful advocate who works to include Deaf people in culture, art and the wider world. She has even performed the American National Anthem in sign language at the Super Bowl, which is football's biggest event in the US, her hope being that it would inspire the many Deaf children watching the game on the TV at home

The English language is like playing one note at a time ...

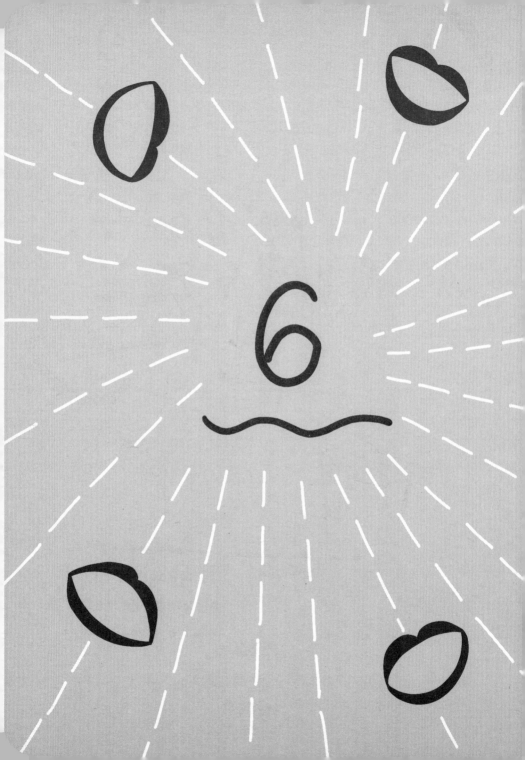

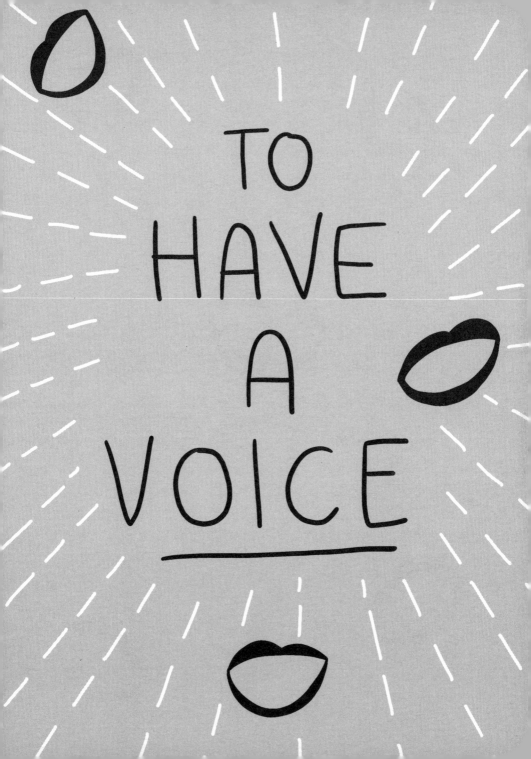

Have you noticed that some people seem to have the gift of speaking? Their words are interesting and engaging. They draw you in. You want to listen to what they are saying. Being able to use your voice in this way is a powerful tool. If you can get people to listen to you, to engage with what you are saying, you can start to make changes and break the mould in all sorts of ways. (Remember that it is really important to be a good listener too.)

Collecting, practising and growing comfortable with words and language is the first step to having and using your voice.

But, you also need to be CONFIDENT and BELIEVE that your voice is worth listening to.

Do you ever feel like yours is not good enough? That your voice, your perspective and your ideas are not interesting or not important. That other people should speak, and you should just listen.

I used to believe this. I would often catch myself thinking that I wasn't good enough, I wasn't interesting, I wasn't important and I shouldn't speak. I spent too much time comparing myself to other people, trying to sound, think, speak and write like them.

Thinking like this is very damaging to your confidence, but one moment completely changed how I thought about myself, and showed me the importance of using my voice.

Have you ever heard of a TED talk? It's a collection of speeches about people's ideas and perspectives, to help change how we view the world. It's difficult to pick a favourite, but I have three.

The first is called *'A LOVE STORY FOR THE CORAL REEF CRISIS'* by **AYANA ELIZABETH JOHNSON**. She is an American marine biologist, which means she studies the oceans and the plants and creatures that live there. In her TED talk, she describes the parrotfish - a species of fish, with mouths that look like parrot beaks. Did you know that they are known as the lawnmowers of the oceans? Or that they poop fine white sand? Or that just before they go to sleep they grow a mucus bubble that completely covers them and masks their scent from predators? I didn't! But although it sounds like parrotfish can look after themselves, they do need our help. With pollution, climate change and plastic in our oceans, there aren't as many fish in the sea as there once were. In her speech Ayana explained that we can use our voices, our choices and put pressure on politicians to make sure that parrotfish continue to swim in the sea!

The second is called *'AN ODE TO LIVING ON EARTH'* by **OLIVER JEFFERS**. He is a writer, artist and illustrator from Northern Ireland. In his TED talk, he describes a conversation between him and his zero-year-old son. Yes, zero. Jeffers tells his son that Earth, our planet, is home to everything we know and have ever heard of. But how can anyone really describe it and how it all works? Its land and seas, a place where time moves fast and slow. A home for people who come in all different shapes, sizes and colours. People who may look different, act different and sound different, but are actually the same. We're all people! So how would you describe Earth? Simply, people live here … a reminder that the obvious things are not always obvious until you think about them.

The third is called *'THE DANGER OF A SINGLE STORY'* by

CHIMAMANDA NGOZI ADICHIE. She is a Nigerian writer who started reading at the age of two. In the books she read, the characters were white with blue eyes, who ate apples and played in the snow. So, when Chimamanda began writing her own stories, her characters were white with blue eyes, who ate apples and played in the snow. But Chimamanda lived in Nigeria, she didn't eat apples, she ate mangoes and she had never seen snow before. She wrote what she read, leading her to believe that the only stories that mattered were those that already existed. Chimamanda reminds us that children with black skin should exist in books and we each have the power to write our own stories.

Those three speeches have been viewed millions of times and have changed how the world thinks about the oceans, the earth and stories.

To my surprise, I was invited to give a TED talk about three years ago. I was asked to speak about my disability and design; the ways in which the world was not built for me. I was a teacher, a writer and an activist … I wasn't a designer. I felt that I wasn't the right person to give the talk, I didn't believe in myself or my experiences.

I said no. I turned TED down.

A moment that changed my life in so many brilliant ways … almost didn't happen! And that was because I didn't think I was good enough.

I didn't believe in myself, not fully, but luckily I told my parents, my siblings and some friends, and they convinced me to change my mind.

When someone gives a TED Talk, they present their speech to a live audience, but they have no script nor is anyone prompting them with the next word or line. Like an actor, you have to perform it from memory.

MY TED TALK

Step One

I need to write my speech. I spend hours looking at a blank page and can't stop thinking, 'What would Ayana, Oliver or Chimamanda write?' I try to think and write like them. I use words and phrases that don't come naturally to me. I want to trick the audience into thinking that I am just like them. I don't want them to know that I am just Sinéad.

I submit the first draft of the talk and the feedback is, 'It doesn't sound like you.'

It doesn't sound like me because I am using other people's words and phrases. I am hiding my experiences, my voice … and me.

Step Two

I start again. This time, I write the speech in my own voice and in my own words. I use language to hold a mirror to my experience, to proudly show the audience who I am. It is honest and it is so much better.

Step Three

The dress rehearsal. I can't remember the speech. My fingers feel like icicles and my pulse is thumping.

I know it. I have memorised it. I know that I know it.
Why can't I remember it on stage when it really matters?

Step Four

Breathe. The back of my neck is hot, my palms are clammy and my hands and voice are shaking. I am so nervous, I can't think of anything but being nervous. I need to do something.

I'm in an accessible bathroom, standing in front of the sink and mirror. I take a deep breath and exhale to lower my shoulders and calm the tension in my neck.

Staring at my reflection, at myself, I say, 'This is your story. No one can tell this story like you, because this is your story. You are good enough just as you are. You are interesting. You are important.'

I take one more deep breath and walk backstage, calming the ball of anxiety that lives in my chest.

One of the stage assistants finds me and says, 'Sinéad, you're up next!'

Step Five
Show time.

I can feel the heat of the spotlights. I can make out the silhouettes of the people sitting in the first few rows, but everyone else fades into the darkness.

I start speaking, narrating my physical journey from my home in Ireland to New York. I can feel the energy from the audience, they want to hear my story. They laugh, they gasp and they become quiet and thoughtful in parts too.

As I utter my final words, the audience erupts in applause. It gets louder, and just when I think it will end, it keeps on going. I smile so hard, a grin stretches across my whole face.

I HAVE DONE IT!

My TED talk is called, **'Why Design Should Include Everyone'** and it has been viewed online over one million times, which is almost the population of Dublin, or Ottawa, or Birmingham, or Adelaide. It changed my life, not because so many people watched it, but because finally, I started to believe in myself.

But it nearly didn't happen for a number of reasons:

✳ I was nervous to try something new and I didn't want to fail or embarrass myself. I said no because it was easier to believe that I couldn't do it, rather than taking a risk and giving it a try.

✳ I tried to be someone else, and tried writing something that wasn't true to me and who I am.

✳ I put too much pressure on myself and almost caved to my nervousness. I panicked and worried, and panicked and worried.

Now that you know what not to do, it's your turn … if I can do it, you can too.

FINDING YOUR VOICE

Imagine YOU were asked to give an important talk, or a speech to a HUGE audience, about something that you care passionately about. It sounds scary, but you've got this!

First, pick your topic. You can talk about anything you believe in or want to fight for. That could be climate change, feminism, accessibility, or even putting an end to homework.

Second, write the speech in your own words and from your own experience. You don't have to be an expert in everything, just believe and remember that you are an expert in yourself.

Third, find your audience. They could be a parent, a brother, a sister, a friend, even the mirror in your bathroom, or if you're feeling very brave, your school assembly.

Fourth, stand proudly in the spotlight and deliver the speech knowing that your voice is important, that who you are and the differences that define you are worth being proud of.

Five, let the audience get to know you, and allow them to be moved by your words and your experience. Wait for the applause. Your voice has been heard, and this is the first step towards making changes happen.

──────────────── **TIP** ────────────

If you feel nervous, remind yourself:

'This is **YOUR STORY**.
No one can tell this story
like you, because this is
your story. You are interesting.
You are important. You are
enough just as **YOU** are.'

UNSUNG HEROES: THE PEOPLE YOU'RE NOT TAUGHT ABOUT AT SCHOOL

ADWOA ABOAH is a British-Ghanaian fashion model and a mental health advocate. She has been on the cover of Vogue, the lifestyle and fashion magazine, and has modelled on the catwalks of London, Paris, New York and Milan. But depression has always been a part of her life, even though from the outside, it isn't possible to tell or maybe even imagine. Adwoa realised that there was power in bringing people together and in finding space to talk about the things that worry, concern and upset us. She knew that ultimately she wasn't the only person who needed to look after her mental health, but that by sharing stories and learning from each other, people would discover that they were not alone. Adwoa uses her voice to help people find a safe way to talk about their mental health, their ambitions and their dreams, to help them break the mould.

By sharing
STORIES ... people
would discover
THEY were
NOT ALONE

Finding your voice takes time. You might not yet know what you believe in, or what you want to change. Or you might be very confident and already be convincing people to think differently about the world around them. But if you have a hiccup and your confidence takes a dive, remind yourself of how brilliant, important and valuable you are. Take another look at your lists, and remember the words of Michelle Obama,

'YOUR **STORY** IS WHAT YOU HAVE, WHAT YOU WILL **ALWAYS** HAVE. IT IS SOMETHING TO **OWN**.'

MICHELLE OBAMA

Giving a speech is just one way to use your voice and your story, but if that doesn't sit comfortably with you, there are so many other ways that you can be seen and heard. If you realise that your schoolyard or playground is polluted with litter, you can organise a tidy-up, beginning with yourself, then asking a few friends to join, then inviting your neighbours and your community.

If you feel passionate about something and think that change needs to happen, you can make a difference. Say for example, you think that one day a week everyone in your class should try to eat a vegetarian lunch. You could start a petition, which is a list of names of people who agree with you. You might sign it first, then your friends, then the other students who are older and younger than you. You can then give this to your head teacher, or whoever it is that organises the menu at school. The petition is proof that it's not only you who cares about this issue, but lots of other people too. It might be enough to change the rules ... and even your lunch meals too!

Finding and using your voice is so important, and it has never been more important. Whether you use that voice to give a speech on stage, to make a difference to your local community, to change the rules, or even to stand up for a friend if they're being bullied, there are so many ways that you can make a difference.

BELIEVE
IN YOURSELF
AND TRUST
THAT YOU
CAN DO IT!

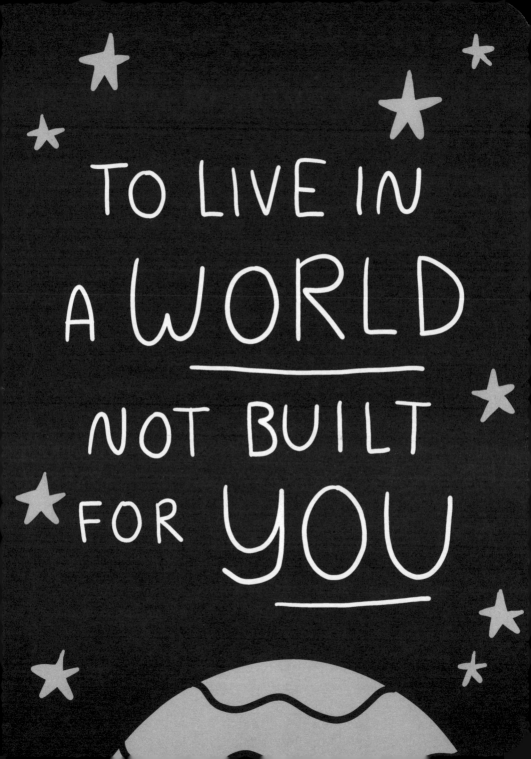

So far, we've explored the things we like about ourselves, we've mapped out our differences and the similarities that unite us. We have worked on ways to be curious, and to be kind, and we've discovered how we can use language and our voice for good in the world. But, now is the time to stop focusing inward, to stop thinking about what we can do differently, and to look around to start thinking about how the world should change for us.

In chapter 2, I told you a story about how I was given an opportunity to be taller. To change my body to fit with the measurements of the world. I chose not to have that surgery, it wasn't the right choice for me then, and even more now. You see, I don't think of my body as something that makes me less of a person, nor do I see it as something that should make me feel embarrassed. I'm not disabled simply because I'm a little person, I'm disabled because when the world was being designed, it was not created for people who look like me.

For a second, imagine what the world would look like if it was designed for me.

Think of your house, how might it look different? What about the playground? Or a shop? Or a bike? Or an aeroplane? Or a car?

If the world was designed for me, if everything was built for little people, it's likely that everyone else would be disabled.

Well, maybe not everyone. I guess because you and me are close to the same height, by design, my world would include you too. It would be our world.

But as you get older and taller, your back would begin to ache as you would need to bend down to climb through small door frames or fill the dishwasher, or wash your hands in smaller sinks.

Trying to wash my hands and use the toilet in a public bathroom is when I remember that the world was not designed for me. I enter the bathroom, queue for a cubicle, go inside ... and already there's a problem.

The lock is too high for me to reach up and close it. I can't climb up onto the toilet and reach over to close it either. It's too far, I'd fall.

I have a routine that I've practised in bathrooms all over the world. Firstly, I look for a bin. I turn it upside down, stand on it and hope that it can bear my weight. Secondly, if there is no suitable bin, I hope that reaching high and using my phone to thwack the lock closed will work. Thirdly, if I still can't reach the lock, I take off my jacket and bag and lay them on the ground of the cubicle just at the divide between the door and the wall, hoping that someone outside will notice that I'm inside and won't try to come in. But, if there is no suitable bin, if my phone won't work and if I'm not wearing a coat or a bag… I ask a stranger for help.

I open the door and scan the people to see who looks the kindest, though it's difficult to tell. I'll pick someone and say, 'Hi, I'm Sinéad. I am sorry to bother you, but I can't reach the lock to close the door and I really need to use the bathroom, would you mind standing outside the door, to make sure no one comes in, please?'

'Sure, no problem.'

It's what they always say. My independence is rooted in strangers' kindness.

I use the toilet and leave the cubicle. I need to wash my hands.

But the sink, soap dispenser and hand dryer are all out of reach. I imagine that you have experienced this too, given that most bathrooms are built for average-height adults. I've learned to carry hand sanitiser with me to ensure that my hands are clean, even when I can't reach the sink.

Often, I'll visit the disabled or accessible bathroom just to wash my hands because there, the sink, soap dispenser and hand-dryer are all lower, as is the lock on the door. But, the toilet is too high for me. It is designed at that height so that wheelchair users can transfer from their chair to the toilet with ease. It makes sense and is necessary, but it shows that even when we design for disabled people, we sometimes still only design for one kind of disability.

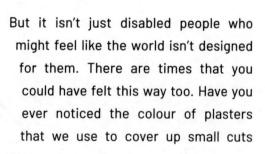

But it isn't just disabled people who might feel like the world isn't designed for them. There are times that you could have felt this way too. Have you ever noticed the colour of plasters that we use to cover up small cuts and grazes? The people who design these plasters say that the colour is nude, by which they mean it's the colour of skin. But, whose skin? The colour of people's skin can vary so much and these 'nude' plasters are really only nude for one particular skin colour. It's the same with ballet slippers, underwear and lipsticks. How do you think it would make a dancer feel when they want to wear a pair of ballet slippers that match their skin colour, but the 'nude' shoes don't match their skin at all? Although this may not seem important to people whose skin colour matches this definition of 'nude', it can make anyone who doesn't have white skin feel as though they aren't 'normal'. Whether it's public bathrooms, clothing, plasters, ballet slippers, or the design of buildings, the way the world is built can either make life easy or much harder for some people.

BE AN ARCHITECT FOR THE DAY

Now that we have learned about the importance of design and have seen the ways in which it can include or exclude people, it's your turn to

DREAM, IMAGINE and build a BETTER WORLD.

But, before you get started, remember that people come in lots of different shapes and sizes and to accommodate everyone, or as many different people as possible, you need to be creative. Can you design ballet shoes or plasters that are engineered to change to the skin colour of the person wearing them? Can you create sinks that move up and down - either automatically or manually – to adjust to the height of the user?

Tomorrow is your first day in this new job as an architect for the world. You can completely redesign it. Are you ready? Be bold and think outside the 'norm'. Grab some pencils, crayons, big pieces of paper and start designing your world.

Can you build a playground that is safe, fun and exciting for all children to use? Can you create clothes that alter and change, as if by magic? Can you solve the problems of the future?

The future will be ACCESSIBLE

UNSUNG HEROES: THE PEOPLE YOU'RE NOT TAUGHT ABOUT AT SCHOOL

ZAHA HADID was a British-Iraqi architect who showed the world a whole new way to design buildings. Zaha's designs can be seen in London, Glasgow, Rome, Vienna, New York, Michigan, Beijing, Seoul, Baku and more. She looked at the world from a different angle and always created her buildings through this viewpoint. Her style was called 'deconstructivism', which means that she pulled things apart to figure out new ways to put them together again! In her drawings, Zaha's lines and structures were never predictable, with her buildings curving into the sky almost as if they were built by magic.

Zaha was the first woman to receive the Royal Gold Medal from the Royal Institute of British Architects. Zaha wasn't afraid to speak out, but she believed in herself and worked hard to make her mark on the world and effect real changes. She didn't let the world change who she was.

An ARCHITECT who showed the world a new way to DESIGN buildings

CREATING A CLASSROOM

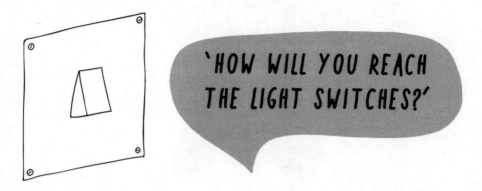

Imagine your classroom. Can you visualise it? Now imagine that I am your teacher in that classroom. What would be out of my reach? What might I need help with?

In my class, I couldn't close the blinds, or open a window, or turn a light switch on. I also wasn't tall enough to display my students' artwork. This didn't make me a bad teacher, in fact, I was a great teacher. The classroom just wasn't designed for me... But, it didn't mean that it couldn't be changed, or that I wouldn't find a new way to do things.

The other question that people sometimes asked me about, was how did I think my students would respond to me, as I would be smaller than them? The thing I found out was that it really didn't matter about the difference in our heights; the important thing was that I showed interest in the things they liked and listened to their point of view, and in return they were happy to listen to me and to help me make the classroom a safe and accessible place for everyone.

In my classroom, my students loved football and even though I didn't like it as much as they did, it was important to them, so it became important to me too. Every evening I watched the match highlights, learning who scored a goal and when, or who was fouled, and if the referee was out of order! Whether it was Manchester United or the US Women's Team at the World Cup, I didn't understand all of it, but I tried. My students laughed at me when I pronounced Megan Rapinoe's last name wrong (it's Re-pee-no, by the way), and they were impressed when I told them that I admired Mohamed Salah. We created a common bond and in return for me learning about their interests and valuing them, my students began helping me too. They helped me with the light switches, the blinds, rearranging the desks so I could

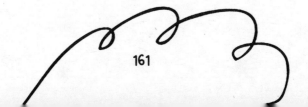

see everyone and they could all see me, and hanging up the artwork. We were able to work together to make the classroom an accessible place where everyone felt respected.

ACCESSIBILITY

is a noun to describe when the world and different products are designed for disabled people. Some examples are a ramp leading up to the bus doors, which makes a bus accessible for a wheelchair user, and bumpy surfaces on the ground at train stations or by busy roads, which make the streets accessible for people who are blind or visually impaired. Even not wearing perfumes or scented fragrances can make the world more accessible for autistic people.

Living in a world that is not designed for you is tough, but by respecting other people and working with them, you can change this. Listen to other people, and they will listen to you. Don't be afraid to ask for help or to offer help. Learn about other people's interests and beliefs, be curious about what makes each of us different, believe in yourself and your ideas, and use your voice to stand up for what you and others might believe in. Break that mould - just because the world has always been one way, doesn't mean you can't change it for the better. And it all starts with embracing differences and realising there is no one quite like you.

THE WORLD SHOULD CHANGE FOR YOU

There are moments when we all feel left out, especially in school. Was there ever a birthday party in your class and it felt like everyone else was invited but you? Maybe you struggle with maths or English and need extra support, and it seems like everyone else around you seems to understand it straight away? Maybe everyone has a bike but you can't afford one? Maybe you've just arrived in a new country and don't speak the language as well as other people? Maybe you're D/deaf* and others don't speak your language? Maybe you're not as fast at running as the other kids in your class? Maybe you find loud noises and/or bright lights difficult - and become overwhelmed when it's too much? Maybe you just feel different, but don't really know why ...

*I use the term 'D/deaf' here because 'Deaf', with a capitalised D, is used to describe sign language users. Whereas 'deaf', with a lower case d, is used to describe those who are hard of hearing, but have English as their first language and who lipread and/or use hearing aids.

Sometimes the world can feel like it is not built for you. It can make you feel alone and even allow you to believe that it will always be this way. The world was designed for a one size fits all; but it doesn't fit me, and maybe not you. But why don't we change it? Why don't we design a world where everyone feels included and connected? It's possible.

So, what could you do? If you notice that your classroom library is filled with books where the characters don't look like you, you could speak to your teacher, ask them to introduce some new stories. You could also bring in a book from home, or your local library, and read it to your class. You could learn a new language, perhaps sign language, or share the languages you do speak with your friends. If you love sport, try to be aware that not everyone might run as fast as you, and you could offer your friends a head start, or if one friend doesn't want to or can't run, you could ask them to be the referee. If you're watching a film and there are lots of loud noises and flashing lights, you could make sure that everyone is comfortable with the volume and if a friend is sensitive to the lights, you could choose to watch something else – a film or TV show that everyone can enjoy.

The world is sort of like clay, it has taken its current shape because of the people who have moulded it. But this design doesn't work for everyone, so we need to be brave, curious and confident that we can remould and redesign the world, to fit and accommodate you, me and everybody.

GO ON, START TO BREAK THE MOULD!

TO BE

SEEN

WHAT IS YOUR DREAM?

If you could do or be anything, what would it be?

A dancer

A teacher

A NURSE

A poet

A set designer

A SCIENTIST

A computer programmer

An athlete

Have your dreams changed? Have any come true? Do some still feel impossible?

For a very long time, one of my dreams was to be part of the fashion industry. But when I looked at magazines or went to a shop, I felt excluded. It felt like fashion didn't know that I existed. I wanted to change that.

I remember being at the shops and gliding my hand through the different fabrics. I loved the idea that you could put one of these pieces of clothing on and it would transform how the world looked at you, but also, make you feel differently about yourself.

As a little person, I love fashion as it allows me to communicate who I am to the world. Often, when people look at me, they have assumptions about what I can or cannot do, because of my disability. Imagine if I wore a full-length sequin dress in the middle of the bread aisle at the supermarket, now *that* would give them a completely different idea about who I am and what I can do.

... Although maybe not in a good way!

I was a teenager when I first went shopping with my sisters. They're not little people but they are younger than me. I remember watching them dance between the rails, the changing rooms and the cash register without the challenges I had. They could reach

everything and they didn't have to think about shopping the way I had to.

In a shop, I struggle to reach most things and even though I love fashion, I find the act of looking for clothes upsetting. There is so little that I can do on my own without help and so many of the clothes are not designed for me.

My sisters could pick up a new pair of jeans and wear them straight away, and buy t-shirts and shoes that didn't make them feel younger than they were. It became obvious to me that I wouldn't get to wear the clothes and shoes that I dreamed of; they didn't fit, and often, they didn't exist.

My interest changed from being concerned about my wardrobe, to learning about how the fashion industry worked.

Who were the people with POWER? How could FASHION be more INCLUSIVE? How could I help make this happen?

MAKING THE WORLD MORE INCLUSIVE

Is there something in the world that you want to see changed to be more inclusive? Why not write down your ideas in a notebook on how this might happen and who you could talk to, to help you start making these changes. You could include diagrams of your design ideas too. Writing about your own experiences and sharing them (even if it is just with your friends and family) can give you the courage to make changes happen, to be brave, to believe in yourself and to achieve your most impossible dreams.

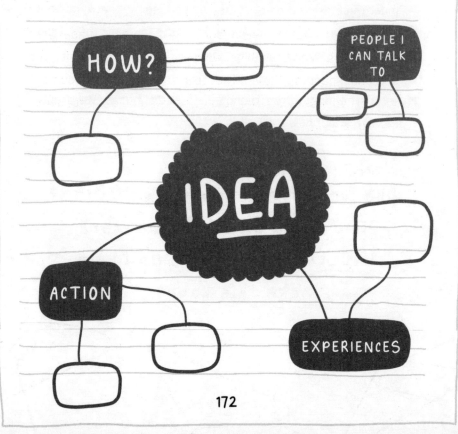

Every evening, I would have conversations with my parents and siblings about the issues in the fashion industry. My family loves me. They did not love these conversations.

'Is there anyone else that you can talk to about this?' I remember them asking. None of my friends cared about fashion in the way that I did. I needed an outlet. A place for me to have a voice. A space for me to change the world.

I found it, but not where I was expecting ...

When I was in university, one of our lecturers made a suggestion. He advised us to create a blog, which is similar to a website, it's a personal space on the internet to write about and document whatever you choose. He said that we could write about anything ... so I wrote about fashion.

This moment changed my life.

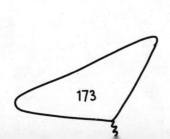

WHO IS NOT IN THE ROOM?

Writing words and publishing them made me feel strong and confident and valued. I was documenting my experiences of feeling excluded from the fashion industry. I wasn't sure if anyone would read it, because I thought it was just me that had been forgotten. But, I received emails and comments from many different people who had different types of bodies, beliefs and interests, from all over the world. They said they felt excluded

too. These were Black people, people of colour, disabled people or plus-sized people. So many people were missing from the pages of magazines and fashion runways, their voices were silenced, their experiences were made invisible and by leaving them out, by not including them, the world told them that there was only one definition of beauty and style. The definition was white skin, tall, thin and non-disabled.

But, once you begin to take note of exclusion, your awareness grows. It wasn't just the fashion industry that made so many people feel left out. It was in books, on television, in films, in boardroom offices, in sports teams and even in government. It made me ask the questions, 'Who was not in the room?' and 'How do we change that?'

With so much to change, it can feel overwhelming, but the key to using your voice and being an activist is not tackling all of the world's problems at once, but figuring out where you can have the most impact.

Choose something you feel <u>PASSIONATE</u> about – it is always easier to speak or write about something you love.

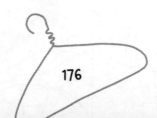

For me, that was within the fashion industry. At a fashion show, I met Edward Enninful, the newly appointed Editor-in-Chief of the fashion magazine, British *Vogue*. He was the first Black man to ever hold that title, the most important position at the magazine, and already, he was finding ways to reflect different types of people and different kinds of bodies within the magazine.

It took me a while to work up the confidence to go and speak to him, but just as I could see him leaving, I went over and tugged on the sleeve of his jacket. Nervously I told him I wanted to talk about how we can make fashion more inclusive of people with disabilities. He agreed and we started working together. I wrote lots of articles and began working within fashion companies to help them think about designing clothes for disabled people, making their shops more accessible and their fashion shows more inclusive.

For me, being able to wear a Burberry trench coat, a silk Prada floral dress, a black Gucci tuxedo, a Givenchy couture gown with a cape, carrying a Louis Vuitton handbag and wearing custom Ferragamo high-heels was the stuff of my dreams. My dreams came true. For you, it might be being able to wear your favourite sports gear or seeing more people like you starring in films,

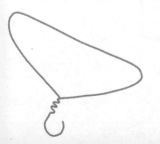

TV shows and musicals, or sitting in government, or working as a doctor, a teacher or a lawyer, or playing in a pop band, or representing your country in a big sporting event.

For the first time,

I UNDERSTOOD HOW IT FELT WHEN YOU WORE CLOTHES THAT FIT YOUR BODY.

My wardrobe full of clothes was my armour, protecting me from the weather and challenging what people thought when they looked at me.

UNSUNG HEROES: THE PEOPLE YOU'RE NOT TAUGHT ABOUT AT SCHOOL

KERBY JEAN-RAYMOND is a Haitian-American fashion designer. His brand is called Pyer Moss and it is proudly inspired by Black heritage and culture. Kerby hasn't always felt included in fashion. There are not many designers who look like him, but he never allowed that to extinguish his dreams. He is described as the designer who is changing the world in how we think about fashion, and he is a person who stands up for others, no matter the cost.

Kerby's designs are a commentary on the world around us: whether it is Black Lives Matter, or the importance of celebrating Black joy, Kerby understands that fashion is important because we all wear clothes and what we wear can narrate to the world who we are and what we might stand for.

Kerby believes that if people don't want to include you, you should not change who you are to fit in, but proudly do your own thing and have confidence in yourself and what you believe in.

YOU SHOULD NOT CHANGE who you are to FIT IN, but proudly DO YOUR OWN THING

181

But a moment that topped even this fantastic feeling of being able to wear the clothes I'd always dreamed of wearing, came when I was asked to feature on the cover of *Vogue*, alongside fourteen other women in their 'forces for change' edition.

I got to dress in a black Prada dress and lace cape, with a wind machine blowing my curled hair! I twirled and the dress spun, and I remember thinking how if my teenage self could see me now, how proud and thrilled she would have been to feel represented. Here I was as an activist for change, celebrating difference, having my voice heard and truly breaking the mould!

I was the first little person on the cover of *Vogue*. Ever.

Walking past my local bookshops and newsagents, I could see the magazine on the shelves and glimpse my photo. It was surreal, exciting and a little overwhelming. But the moments that I have been most proud of came later. Moments when I realised the power of feeling represented, but not just for me, for others too. When the magazine launched, kind people sent photographs of their children and of themselves clutching the magazine. It mattered, but even more because these were little people. Little people who may never have thought that their bodies, that their disability, would be seen as beautiful or stylish in fashion.

But these children and adults now know that they are beautiful, stylish and cool. In many ways, they've always known, but the power of seeing a photograph of someone who looked like them, in a magazine as important as *Vogue*, proved to themselves and, more importantly, to the world, that they don't need to change who they are. That they are enough – just as they are.

Being able to see yourself reflected in fashion magazines or in films or television shows, means that you feel represented. Your experience and your difference is visible, not just to you, but to the world. Representation and visibility are so important, because without words, it gives everyone the confidence to achieve our dreams. For too long, people like me, and maybe you, didn't feel represented, or that our experiences were visible, but finally, that's beginning to change. I've spoken about fashion and disability, because they are the things that reflect my experience and the things that I can speak most effectively on. But there are so many other groups of people who are under-represented in so many different places.

For you, that might be in books. Maybe the books you read at school are mostly by white writers and you don't feel represented, or the characters rarely have a disability and your experience is

invisible. Thinking about what Chimamanda said in her TED talk, there is often only one type of story or one type of character, but you can change that. You can create a petition for your class, your school and your community, to push for more inclusive books. You can ask your teachers to read and show you more diverse stories and you can write your own. You could ask your parents to help you write a blog or vlog (a video diary). Your story has never been more important. Share it with your friends and family. Research organisations and people that share your passions and ideals. You never know, an e-mail or letter to one of them could be the start of something amazing!

There is a phrase that says,

**'IF YOU CAN SEE IT,
YOU CAN BE IT'.**

For many of us, the possibility of seeing people who look like us in the places that we wish we could be might not happen today, or tomorrow. But, please do not give up. This does not make your dream impossible, because even though there may not be a role model for you, you can be that person for someone else. That might mean one day appearing on the cover of a magazine, or changing the types of stories that appear in your classroom

184

library. But, it might also mean being the first person in your family to go to university, or the only kid from your community to ever play in the Premier League.

You may not believe it now, but in a few years, somewhere in the world, there will be a child who says, 'I want to be just like them'. They'll be talking about YOU!

MOMENT TO A MOVEMENT

Remember that list I asked you to write earlier? The one where you thought about your likes and dislikes, your hobbies and your interests and what makes you YOU? Dig it out now and have another look at what you wrote down. What's your 'Vogue' moment? In other words, what's your ultimate goal, the dream that you want to achieve? Every morning, do you wake up wanting to be an actor, or a scientist, or an author or a doctor?

Whatever you wish to do, change, or be is possible, but the lack of representation and visibility makes it a little more challenging. Don't give up. You and me, we've got this!

So let's get started. Are you ready?

(1)   Do you feel represented? By that I mean, when you watch films, or television programmes, or see scientists and doctors in the media, or in a lab and a hospital, do the people already working in those careers look like you? If not, it's important to remember that this doesn't mean that your dream is impossible. We just have to change the world. Easy. So, let's think - what are the steps that you can take to make sure that you're included?

(2)   If you do feel represented, that's great! Making your dream a reality starts right now. But, taking our place in the world is more than just making a difference that benefits ourselves.

Who isn't represented and included? Who isn't yet in these rooms? What can you do to make sure that more people are included?

Of course, you can't change the world in one day, so start by finding out as much information as you can about the things you care about and want to change (whether that's for yourself and others like you, or for other people that aren't included). Talk about these things with your friends and family, and maybe ask your teacher if you can do a presentation to your class. You could contact organisations or people who are already activists for your cause. You could volunteer your time to a charity or initiative.

CHANGE takes time, but with DETERMINATION you can start to make a DIFFERENCE now.

The world can be a confusing place. It's constantly changing, sometimes for good reasons and sometimes not. But every act matters and you can use your words and actions to make a difference each day.

Think of Greta Thunberg who changed the world by skipping school. (This is not the point in the book where I recommend you skip school!) But, she knew that our world was in danger, that we needed to do something to help our planet and environment. She started a weekly protest. Greta's protest took place in her home in Sweden. Once a week she would sit outside government buildings with a sign that read, **Skolstrejk för klimatet:** School Strike for Climate. She encouraged other children to care about the environment and inspired them to use their voices too. Because of her, hundreds of thousands of young people, all over the world, have skipped school to lead and follow their friends in a climate strike for the planet. Maybe you took part, maybe you joined them. Greta used her voice and dared to break the mould.

Think of Amariyanna Copeny, also known as Little Miss Flint, she changed the world by writing a letter. (This is the point in the book where I recommend you to start writing letters...) Amariyanna wrote a letter to Barack Obama, who at the time was

President of the United States. She wrote to tell him about the dirty and dangerous water in her hometown of Flint. You couldn't drink it, you couldn't wash with it – it was a crisis. After receiving Amariyanna's letter, Barack Obama made sure that Flint had the money and the resources it needed to make the water safe and clean again. All because of one girl, and one letter.

So, what are the steps that you can take to CHANGE THE WORLD?

That's not an easy question, because there isn't just one answer. It will take time for you to find your way: maybe you'll create petitions, march on protests, write a letter, raise money for a great cause, create a blog, change the law or make a documentary. We each have to find our own way that's shaped by who we are, what we believe in and how we see the world.

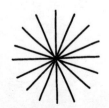

193

For me, I like to make a difference by asking questions.

The status quo includes only one type of person, or one type of body, because people in power and those responsible for making decisions often only see the world from their perspective. Even though some of them might not be deliberately excluding others, they often forget that all sorts of other people exist who are different to them.

To explain what I mean, let me tell you a story based in Edinburgh in Scotland. I was asked to participate in an exhibition called 'Body Beautiful', it was about diversity in fashion, it would represent different shapes, bodies, genders, disabilities and religions. I was asked if I would lend some of my clothes to the exhibition, but I wondered how would they be displayed?

I learned that my clothes would dangle from the ceiling, but all of the other garments would be displayed on mannequins. A mannequin of a little person did not exist. Not yet, anyway.

'How do we create a mannequin?' I asked.

Just by asking that question (and lots of hard work), I created the world's first mannequin of a little person. I had my body cast in

plaster and rubber and I will never forget seeing my mannequin for the first time.

I had spent my **WHOLE LIFE** seeing only **ONE KIND** of body represented; one that was tall and thin. <u>**ASKING QUESTIONS**</u> and <u>**CHALLENGING**</u> the **STATUS QUO** changed that and, in turn, <u>**CHANGED**</u> the fashion industry.

But, what's your way?

Could you paint a portrait of someone you admire or are inspired by? Maybe it's a body or a difference that hasn't been visible before. Could you write a letter to change the law, or to bring attention to what's happening to you? Could you be a storyteller and bring characters and people to life? Could you be a world leader, a person who will make laws to make your home, community and country a better, safer, more representative place for everyone to live and succeed?

Begin by **ASKING QUESTIONS**,
and then follow this up with
a **POSITIVE ACTION**,
be it a portrait, a letter,
a petition or some of the
ideas pictured here!

UNSUNG HEROES: THE PEOPLE YOU'RE NOT TAUGHT ABOUT AT SCHOOL

NABIL SHABAN is a British-Jordanian actor and writer who created the Graeae Theatre Company, a place where disabled artists and actors can discover and grow their talent. From Doctor Who to Hamlet, Nabil has performed on stage, on television and in films too.

As a disabled man, he understands the importance of representation and how meaningful it is for disabled people to have space to write and tell their own stories. He also knows how important it is to inspire younger disabled people to believe that they have a right to be an actor and a writer too.

...inspire YOUNGER DISABLED PEOPLE to BELIEVE that they have a RIGHT to be an actor and a writer too.

ENOUGH AS YOU ARE

Thinking about changing the world is exciting and inspiring. There is so much potential and the world is yours for the taking! But, when everything seems possible, where do you start?

For me, I sit with a piece of paper and in the centre I draw a bubble and write the words describing my dream. Around the bubble, I then write all of the steps and ways that will bring me closer to that dream. So, for fashion that might be: reading articles, learning about the industry, interviewing people I admire and being brave and saying hello. There is never just one way to do something.

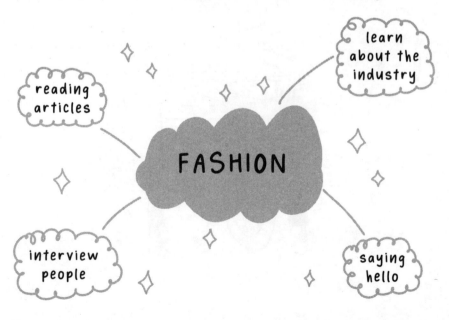

But, on your journey towards changing the world, there is something you should know. There will be times where you will feel low, where it would be easier to stop and do something else, and you will question whether you are good enough. If this happens, remember, your dreams are important and interesting, even when they seem impossible. Change doesn't happen overnight, but as a natural changemaker, you are having an impact every day. You are already shaping your friends, your family, your school, your community and your country.

We are all natural changemakers and every day, we can make an impact.

We already have all of the necessary SKILLS within ourselves. We just need to PRACTISE and to BELIEVE IN OURSELVES.

AN EXERCISE IN CHANGING THE WORLD

On the days I'm feeling powerless, or if change feels impossible, I find thinking about the following questions can help me focus. They remind me of what matters and re-energise me to try, and try again. They might help you too!

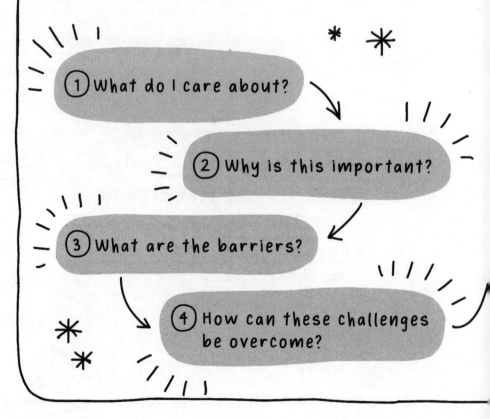

1. What do I care about?

2. Why is this important?

3. What are the barriers?

4. How can these challenges be overcome?

5 What skills do I have to help overcome these hurdles?

6 Who else is advocating for these issues?

7 How could we work together?

8 What does progress mean?

9 How am I bringing other people with me?

10 How do I inspire others to do the same?

MAKING AN UNEQUAL WORLD EQUAL

Can you remember your school Sports Day? There were so many different races and obstacle courses, maybe you played football or rounders or ran in a relay race too.

When I was in primary school, I loved Sports Day. I loved it because my teachers and my classmates made a huge effort to make sure that I could participate fairly.

In every race, I would be given a head start. The teacher would blow the whistle twice; the first time for me to run as fast I could, and the second whistle for the rest of my class. The first year it happened, a couple of the girls asked why, as they felt I was being given an unfair advantage.

My teacher explained that the world isn't designed equally. We don't experience it in the same way.

I couldn't run as fast as the other girls in my class. I was smaller than them and it took a lot more steps for me to run from the start to the finish line. Our effort wasn't the same. The head start made it more equal and more fair. By my teacher blowing the whistle earlier for me, it gave me time to bridge the inequality. It redesigned an unequal world to be more fair.

My teacher and my friends noticed that me trying to run at the same time as everyone else meant that I was disadvantaged, exhausted and embarrassed. So they changed the rules of the race. They were giving me an opportunity to participate equally. Simple things like this made a huge difference.

Have you ever heard of the words 'privilege' and an 'ally'?

Privilege means that you have an advantage. An advantage means you have a more favourable position or that some things may be easier for you. But if you have less of an advantage, you are in a less favourable position and some things may be more difficult for you.

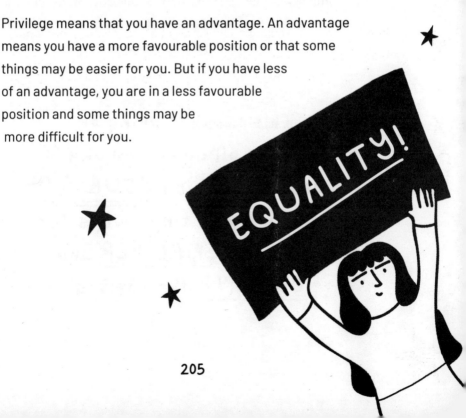

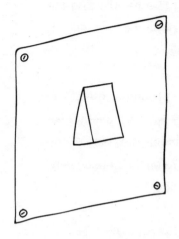

So, what kind of privileges might you have? Well, if you're not disabled, the world is more likely to be designed for you. This gives you an advantage because you don't have to spend time, or energy, thinking about reaching light switches, or wondering how you might wash your hands independently. The ability to not have to think about it at all is an enormous advantage.

But it's important that you are aware of this advantage, and that you use it to make the world fairer and more equal - in the same way that my teacher and friends did at Sports Day.

This is what being an **ALLY** is all about. An ally is someone who is on **YOUR SIDE**. Someone who finds ways for people to **EMPOWER** and **EDUCATE** themselves.

It is a person who uses their voice, not just to speak for themselves, but to stand with others, those who feel less represented and maybe have less advantage.

For example, can you remember a time where you've been in the playground and another kid has called someone a name, a word that you know is unkind and is being used to hurt that person's feelings? Did you speak up? Did you feel safe or comfortable to say something?

It's not easy, particularly if that person who is calling someone names is our friend. We worry about what they might think of us if we speak up, but by staying silent, we are quietly telling them that we agree with them, that how they are treating another person is okay.

So, let me help.

Imagine that you make a plan with three of your friends to get together on the weekend and do something fun. Two of your friends suggest going to the cinema, and then to bowling and maybe then for food. Everyone is very excited, except one friend. They're now saying that they might not go, even though they couldn't stop talking about how much they were looking forward to spending time together. Quickly you realise that maybe they do want to go, but going to the cinema, then bowling and then for food is expensive. Even though you can afford it, you know that not everyone can afford to do all of those things, especially at once. What do you do?

If it was me, I'd say: 'This weekend is going to be really fun! But, I have a different idea. Why don't you come to my house, we can cook noodles, we can watch a movie and spend some time together.'

The two friends who wanted to go to the cinema, bowling and for food will most likely say yes, because they just want to spend time together, and probably got a little too excited. The friend who changed their mind will come to your house too and you will all have fun! Even though three of you could afford to do all of the activities and it would have been really nice to go, you had the advantage because you could afford it but it didn't feel right to leave one friend out because they couldn't afford to go. Instead, you used your advantage to be an ally and find another way of making sure that you could all have a good time together.

Now, imagine that you are in the playground and are standing with your friends. One of them points to a boy who is minding his own business, and shouts, 'You're gay!'.

Already, you can see that your other friends are looking at their feet, avoiding eye contact, but no one is saying anything. What do you do?

If it was me, I'd say: 'Hey, maybe he is, or maybe he isn't. But, the word gay should not be used as an insult to upset someone, or to make them feel like less of a person.

IT IS OKAY TO BE GAY,

but it is not okay to be cruel and unkind.'

Quickly, your other friends will nod and agree with you. The boy will be grateful you said something and your friends may wish they had been brave too.

Some of us have more of an advantage than others, and there are so many moments when we can be an ally. When thinking about changing the world, and taking our place in it, it's important that we think about the advantage that we have, how we can use this to empower others, and how we can be an ally to our friends, family and strangers who experience the world differently.

You might see someone at school being bullied or being treated unkindly because, in some way, they're different. It might not be safe for you to approach the person who is being unkind, or the bully, but you can tell a teacher or an adult. You can be a friend to the person who is being bullied.

You can also be an ally in the language and actions you choose. You can choose to be respectful, curious and kind to everyone around you. You can choose to make the world a better place.

Why is it important? It's important, because everybody is different. We all need allies and friends to make a world that can sometimes treat people differently, just a little more equal.

UNSUNG HEROES: THE PEOPLE YOU'RE NOT TAUGHT ABOUT AT SCHOOL

JANE FONDA is an American actor and activist. She has been a TV and movie star for over sixty years, but she has also used her influence and fame to help fight for human rights, the environment and other social issues. She is an advocate for changing the things that harm other people and our planet. Jane once said that we are born to be rebels, and has used her voice to fight against wars, and to support feminists and the Black community in the fight for their rights. Jane proves that having power is a privilege but also a responsibility. It is easier to speak up for yourself, and more difficult to do so for someone else - but no matter the risk, doing the right thing has never been more important.

Having power is a PRIVILEGE but also a RESPONSIBILITY

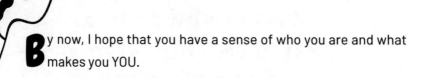

By now, I hope that you have a sense of who you are and what makes you YOU.

I hope that your dreams and ambitions are becoming clearer and that you realise how important and empowering it is to celebrate your differences.

You are almost ready to speak truth to power, a phrase that means challenging the status quo with your story and your perspective. But, before you leap into activism, there is one more thing that you should do.

FIND YOUR PEOPLE.

As you travel along this journey and as you learn to use your voice, being loved, celebrated and supported will be so important to your success.

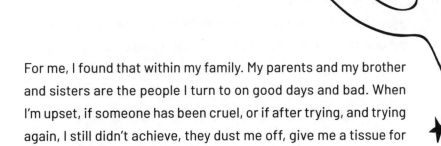

For me, I found that within my family. My parents and my brother and sisters are the people I turn to on good days and bad. When I'm upset, if someone has been cruel, or if after trying, and trying again, I still didn't achieve, they dust me off, give me a tissue for my tears and tell me to try again tomorrow.

But, we don't choose our families and homes aren't always the place where you feel your most comfortable. You might find your people in your grandparents, in your cousins or in your friends from school. It might even be a really supportive teacher from school who helps you realise that you are brilliant. Maybe they will be the people whom you trust with your worries and your dreams. The people who will champion your progress and success - even when YOU don't think it's a big deal.

217

Or maybe you will find that trust and support within yourself. It's possible that right now, you might feel as if 'your people' is just you. But that's okay. You can be the person to remind yourself that you are talented, creative and deserving of every success.

But even when you do find your people, it's important to ALWAYS be KIND to yourself. To TALK to yourself the way you'd expect and hope your CLOSE FRIENDS would talk to you - with KINDNESS, RESPECT and CARE.

Because even if you have all the love, support and care in the world from everyone around you, you have to love yourself too, you have to believe in yourself, in the importance of your dreams and in the power of your voice to really feel comfortable taking your place in the world.

One of my favourite questions to ask is,

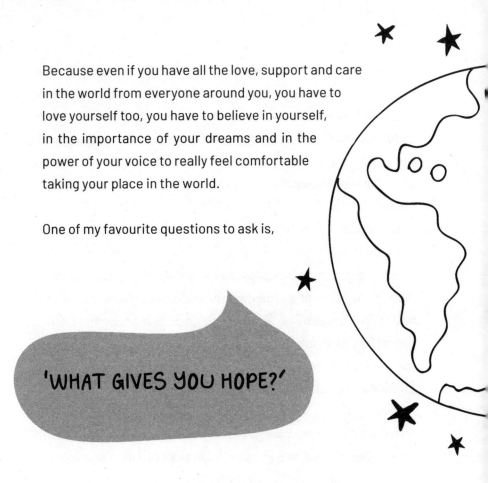

'WHAT GIVES YOU HOPE?'

For me, I have hope in the person reading this book - that's YOU!

The person who is learning to dream boldly and bravely. The person who is proud of themselves and who is becoming more comfortable in their own skin. The person who chooses their words carefully and with kindness. The person who understands the power of their story, the importance of their voice and who above all else knows that they are good enough, just as they are.

I have hope because this person, you, could be a future president, or prime minister. You could be a doctor or a nurse. You could invent a cure for a disease or travel to the moon. You could be a fashion designer or a racing car driver. You could be a chef or a waiter. You could be an activist or a computer programmer. You can be any of these things, no matter what you look like, where you were born, what language you speak at home, if you have a disability or whether you've never felt like you quite fit in.

There was a moment when I could have changed who I was to fit in. I could have grown taller and looked more like everyone else. However, I would still be different, because we are all different. I'm proud of who I have chosen to be. I choose to be kind, to be respectful, to use my voice, to be an ally and to be a changemaker.

So, who do you choose to be?

Whatever path you do choose, remember, you are enough as you are and the world can be changed by you, you don't need to change for the world.

Choose to be you, love what makes you different and grow comfortable in your own skin.

Use your voice to make the world a fairer and more inclusive place. Follow your dreams and help others do the same.

The world is yours. Take your place and …

REFERENCES:

Burke, Sinéad. 'Why Design Should Include Everyone'. Ted. June 2017. https://www.ted.com/talks/sinead_burke_why_design_should_include_everyone/up-next, accessed 23rd July 2020.

Johnson, Ayana Elizabeth. 'A Love Story for the Coral Reef Crisis'. Ted. April 2019. https://www.ted.com/talks/ayana_elizabeth_johnson_a_love_story_for_the_coral_reef_crisis?language=en, accessed 17 July 2020.

Jeffers, Oliver. 'An Ode to Living on Earth'. Ted. April 2020. https://www.ted.com/talks/oliver_jeffers_an_ode_to_living_on_earth, accessed 17 July 2020.

Kim, Christine Sun. 'The Enchanting Music of Sign Language'. Ted. October 2015. https://www.ted.com/talks/christine_sun_kim_the_enchanting_music_of_sign_language/up-next, accessed 23rd July 2020.

Ngozi Adichie, Chimamanda. 'The Danger of a Single Story'. Ted. July 2009. https://www.ted.com/talks/chimamanda_ngozi_adichie_the_danger_of_a_single_story, accessed 17 July 2020.

Obama, Michelle. Becoming. (London: Viking Press, 2018).

RESOURCES:

If you are feeling uncomfortable, overwhelmed or isolated, talking about it and learning about how others experience the world might help. Here are some organisations that support and help with these kinds of conversations:

BelongTo:
Supporting lesbian, gay, bisexual, trans and intersex young people in Ireland. http://www.belongto.org

Black Lives Matter:
Building an anti-racist society, this organisation also creates space for Black imagination and centres Black joy. http://www.blacklivesmatter.com

Bodywhys:
A space where young people who are experiencing avoidant restrictive food disorders can come together and support one another. http://www.bodywhys.ie

Childline:
A counselling service for children and young people, they believe that talking makes us stronger. It does! http://www.childline.org.uk / http://www.childline.ie

Gal-Dem:
A media company sharing the perspectives of women and non-binary people of colour. http://www.gal-dem.com

Little People of Ireland:
A support and educational organisation for little people and their families. http://www.lpi.ie

Mermaids:
A safe place for young trans people to find and support one another. https://www.mermaidsuk.org.uk

ACKNOWLEDGEMENTS:

Writing a book felt like an impossible challenge but working with Laura Horsley and Phoebe Jascourt at Wren & Rook made this dream a reality. They edited this book with such care, openness, curiosity and kindness and they advocated for my vision throughout each paragraph and chapter. Thank you, Laura and Phoebe, for your expertise and friendship.

Throughout this book, Natalie Byrne's powerful and inclusive illustrations tell a new kind of story that will shape the reader for ever. Thank you, Natalie.

Tony and Elaine, you created the foundations that made this book possible. Thank you.

To my friends, the group of people who transform my world view and who (mostly) laugh at my jokes. Thank you, Becky, Colm, Emma, Faran, Georsan, Gina, Gretel, Jamie, Kimberly, Michael, Michelle, Olly, Rowena, Ruth, Siobhán, Sharon, Shaun and Yvonne.

To my siblings, the four people who matter most and whose love, kindness and understanding I am constantly learning from and inspired by. Thank you, Natasha, Niamh, Chris and Chloe.

To my parents, for always believing in me, for encouraging me and for loving me. Thank you.